SHIFTING SANDS

contemporary issues in primary education

Our titles are also available in a range of electronic formats. To order, or for details of our bulk discounts, please go to our website www.criticalpublishing.com or contact our distributor, NBN International, 10 Thornbury Road, Plymouth PL6 7PP, telephone 01752 202301 or email orders@nbninternational.com.

CRITICAL
PUBLISHING

SHIFTING SANDS

contemporary issues in primary education

Gary Pykitt

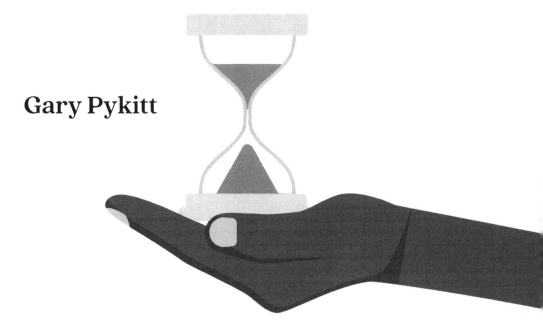

First published in 2019 by Critical Publishing Ltd

Copyright © 2019 Gary Pykitt

British Library Cataloguing in Publication Data
A CIP record for this book is available from the British Library

ISBN: 978-1-912508-53-2

This book is also available in the following e-book formats:
MOBI ISBN: 978-1-912508-54-9
EPUB ISBN: 978-1-912508-55-6
Adobe e-book ISBN: 978-1-912508-56-3

Cartoon illustrations by Élisabeth Eudes-Pascal represented by GCI

Cover and text design by Out of House Limited
Project management by Newgen Publishing UK
Printed and bound in Great Britain by 4edge, Essex

Critical Publishing
3 Connaught Road
St Albans
AL3 5RX

www.criticalpublishing.com

Paper from responsible sources

DEDICATION

I would like to dedicate this book to the memory of my mum, Gail Pykitt, who loved books.

CONTENTS

MEET THE AUTHOR

GARY PYKITT

I am an experienced senior lecturer in primary education at Birmingham City University, specialising in primary history and professional studies. I have worked as a primary-school teacher and a school governor. I am currently vice chair of a multi-academy trust and enjoy regular contact with primary schools to inform my practical understandings of the issues currently impacting upon the primary sector.

ACKNOWLEDGEMENTS

I would like to thank my colleagues who have been so supportive during the writing of this book, and particularly Alison Dolphin and Kirsty Norbury for their school-related advice. I also need to thank my husband, Matt Clay, and my dad, Don Pykitt, for their support during this exciting project.

I. INTRODUCTION

In education, it will constantly feel as if the ground is shifting beneath your feet, and it is challenging to remain up to date with the latest developments and, importantly, how they will impact upon your day-to-day practice. This book raises your awareness of a range of complex and current issues that will impact on your work. There is a highly practical focus: unpicking key elements of legislation and policy. Practical approaches are suggested alongside resources that could be used in the classroom to successfully address the issues. While not necessarily giving you all of the answers, I hope to promote your critical thinking around the issues.

The Teachers' Standards

The Teachers' Standards (Department for Education [DfE], 2011) set out the expectations for teachers in England. This book addresses, particularly, aspects of Part Two:

- treating pupils with dignity, building relationships rooted in mutual respect, and at all times observing proper boundaries appropriate to a teacher's professional position;
- having regard for the need to safeguard pupils' well-being in accordance with statutory provisions;

- showing tolerance of and respect for the rights of others;
- not undermining fundamental British values, including democracy, the rule of law, individual liberty and mutual respect, and tolerance of those with different faiths and beliefs;
- ensuring that personal beliefs are not expressed in ways that exploit pupils' vulnerability or might lead them to break the law;
- having an understanding of, and always acting within, the statutory frameworks that set out their professional duties and responsibilities.

These correlate to:

- Section 2.2 (education systems and professional responsibilities) in the Professional Standards (General Teaching Council for Scotland, 2012);
- the sections pertaining to the reflection on learning, learning outcomes and well-being and exercising corporate responsibility elements of the Professional Standards (Learning Wales, 2018); and
- aspects of the professional values and practice and professional knowledge and understanding sections of the Professional Competencies (General Teaching Council for Northern Ireland, 2011).

It may seem that these elements are what you do every day, but it is important to realise that it is not enough to just know about these elements: you must keep up to date with the developments related to them. Doing this can be challenging, but this book is designed to help you fulfil your statutory duties in line with the latest developments. It signposts key resources to support you in remaining current in a time-efficient manner.

Drivers for change

Issues including mental health and well-being, online safety, prejudice-based bullying and safeguarding among others are all high on the Ofsted and government agenda, frequently featuring in the educational press and sparking debate. Safeguarding legislation is ever-evolving with regular and recent updates to key documentation. The year 2018 marked ten years since the Byron Review, and the evaluation of progress has resulted in some pertinent points being fed forward. There are changes related to relationships and sex education which are due to be implemented from September 2020 to reflect the changing nature of society and the dynamic nature of factors impacting upon this particular issue. With all of these in mind, it is essential that you actively consider how key requirements may be best addressed in the context of your setting.

There is a clear need for trainees' improved understanding of the full spectrum of safeguarding issues in light of Ofsted concerns about trainees' lack of broad and deep understanding of issues upon qualification (Ward, 2017). Issues around social media continue to attract increasing levels of attention. All of this is driving the national agenda related to education.

Ofsted (2013) introduced a key document to guide inspectors in assessing actions taken by schools to prevent and tackle homophobic, biphobic and transphobic bullying, and this has driven the agenda ever since and added impetus to schools' work in this area following the repeal of Section 28 in 2003. Other documentation, including *Preventing and Tackling Bullying* (DfE, 2017) make specific reference to prejudice-based bullying. Religion is often perceived as a barrier to this type of education, but guidance from the Church of England (2017) provides a helpful and positive view. Organisations such as Stonewall and Educate and Celebrate are constantly driving the agenda forward.

Educational disadvantage is an ongoing issue, and research from the Education Endowment Foundation (EEF) continues to inform practice. There is a strong and growing focus on mental health and well-being of both children and teachers.

Inevitably, there are links between all of the issues to be considered, for example the impact of family debt on children's mental health, the impact of hearing about terrorist incidents on children's mental health and issues around social media and well-being.

Audience and features

This book has been designed to have a practical focus with relevance to trainee teachers, teachers, support staff, leaders and governors. It supports your understanding of issues that impact on and underpin the whole curriculum, beyond the individual subject foci that you may sometimes be consumed by. It is intended that this be a constant source of reference to guide and support your practice. Critical questions are included at the end of each chapter and have been designed so that they may be adapted to suit the reader's role. They may be used:

- by leaders to audit current practice to support action planning;
- by trainees, teachers and support staff to support reflection on practice and support professional dialogue and development discussions;
- by governors to provide challenge to leaders in order to support whole-school development.

Links have been made to key current policy to support you in considering aspects of good practice as well as areas for development to ensure not only compliance but the very best outcomes for your pupils. The policy summary contained within each chapter highlights key features of policy and the implications for you in the classroom. Resources have been identified to support you in the practical implementation of the key ideas discussed. Each chapter also contains good practice examples to give you a starting point for addressing the issues in your classroom.

I hope this book provokes thought and enables you to ensure that all of these critical current issues are effectively embedded into your professional practice in a meaningful and time-efficient manner. The issues will no doubt continue to evolve, and it will be interesting to see how these continue to unfold as we move forward.

References

Church of England (2017) Valuing All God's Children. [online] Available at: www.churchofengland.org/sites/default/files/2017-11/Valuing%20All%20God%27s%20Children%27s%20Report_0.pdf (accessed 25 February 2019).

Department for Education (2011) Teachers' Standards. [online] Available at: https://assets.publishing.service.gov.uk/government/uploads/system/uploads/attachment_data/file/665520/Teachers__Standards.pdf (accessed 25 February 2019).

Department for Education (2017) Preventing and Tackling Bullying. London: DfE.

General Teaching Council for Northern Ireland (2011) Professional Competencies. [online] Available at: www.gtcni.org.uk/index.cfm/area/information/page/profstandard (accessed 26 February 2019).

General Teaching Council for Scotland (2012) Professional Standards. [online] Available at: www.gtcs.org.uk/professional-standards/professional-standards.aspx (accessed 26 February 2019).

Learning Wales (2018) Professional Standards. [online] Available at: https://learning.gov.wales/resources/collections/professional-standards?lang=en (accessed 26 February 2019).

Ofsted (2013) Exploring the School's Actions to Prevent and Tackle Homophobic and Transphobic Bullying. [online] Available at: www.schools-out.org.uk/wp-content/files_mf/13843635500FSTEDexploringschoolsactionstopreventhomophobicbullying.pdf (accessed 25 February 2019).

Ward, H (2017) Trainee Teachers Don't Understand Safeguarding Role, Says Ofsted. [online] Available at: www.tes.com/news/trainee-teachers-dont-understand-safeguarding-role-says-ofsted (accessed 25 February 2019).

2. HOW DO I KEEP UP TO DATE WITH MY SAFEGUARDING DUTIES?

Key issues

Safeguarding is at the absolute heart of everything teachers do, with everyone having the responsibility to safeguard and promote the welfare of children (those under 18) and vulnerable adults. Whatever issue you are dealing with, the child must always be at the centre of your thinking. There are regular updates to key documentation, notably *Keeping Children Safe in Education* (DfE, 2018a) that require you to have annual update training. In addition, reflecting the dynamic and fast-paced nature of safeguarding, you also have a responsibility to keep up to date with key developments as they arise. This chapter explains the range of safeguarding issues and considers the practical implications stemming from these. Aspects of safeguarding not discussed within this chapter are online safety (Chapter 3) and issues around the Prevent Duty and tackling radicalisation (Chapter 4).

Safeguarding and child protection

Safeguarding is the overarching term that relates to keeping children safe and ensuring that the context in which they are developing gives them the best start in life. Child protection relates to the *'activity that is undertaken to protect specific children who are suffering, or are likely to suffer, significant harm'* (HM Government, 2018, p 103). Your school will have clear procedures for discussing and reporting any concerns. Any concern about the welfare of any pupil must be discussed with your safeguarding officer or their deputy. It is often difficult to know when a concern is legitimate, which can lead to doubt about whether or not to report. Basically, if you are unsure, you should have a conversation with your safeguarding officer to support your thinking. The DfE (2018a) clearly states that no one individual can have the full picture related to any child, and, therefore, communication and partnership working is essential.

CONTEXTUAL SAFEGUARDING

Contextual safeguarding is new to the *Keeping Children Safe in Education* document (DfE, 2018a) and refers to the wider influences beyond, but not excluding, the school, such as family and home, peer group or neighbourhood, that may impact on children's welfare and safety. These need to be taken into account by you and the safeguarding officer when making any assessments as this will ensure acknowledgement of the full context and bigger picture.

Defining key terms

PHYSICAL ABUSE

This can take a range of forms that cause physical harm. Apart from the obvious examples of hitting, etc, this can also be caused by a parent or carer fabricating symptoms or deliberately inducing illness in a child (DfE, 2018a, p 13). It is often difficult to ascertain if injuries are deliberate or accidental, but repeated unexplained minor injuries can be telltale signs of physical abuse. Physical abuse can also manifest itself in behaviours that can include fear, watchfulness and a desire to please. Frequent absence may also be an indicator. You should never examine a child's injury as only paediatricians are qualified to give a medical diagnosis of injuries. If, during the course of your work, you see a bruise on a non-mobile baby, you must report this immediately as this can be an indicator of physical abuse.

EMOTIONAL ABUSE

Emotional abuse is difficult to identify and is often not as obvious as physical abuse. The DfE (2018, p 14) notes how this can *'involve conveying to a child that they are worthless or unloved, inadequate or valued only insofar as they meet the needs of another person.'* You may notice indicators in children's interactions with their parents. The child may not be able to express their views or may have their self-esteem undermined. This is going to impact on a child's ability to develop and flourish. HM Government (2018) also highlights that emotional abuse can manifest itself in expectations of children that are inappropriate to their stage of development. This can mean that the expectations are above their capability or it can involve the limiting of experiences or *'preventing the child participating in normal social interaction'* (p 104). Signs of emotional abuse will often be behavioural.

Domestic violence is noted in the definition of emotional abuse as children can be distressed by what is happening to their parent or carer. There may be impacts on parenting capacity as well as the potential for children to be affected in some way, physically or emotionally, by the violence. Emotional abuse is not a one-off disagreement between a child and their parents or carers; it is an ongoing thing, and records are important here in building up a complete picture.

Good practice example

MODELLING APPROPRIATE RELATIONSHIPS

It may be difficult for children to recognise what is appropriate conduct within a relationship and what is not. Role play is a good opportunity to develop this understanding. As far as possible, distance this from actual experiences encountered by the children.

You could provide the children with various scenarios that engage them in considering how to react to situations: for example, you are helping somebody get ready for a party at home and help by going and collecting things. When you return, you have forgotten one or two things. Children consider the scenario from the various perspectives within it and consider what would be an appropriate reaction from their relevant character and what would be inappropriate.

Engage the wider group in explaining and justifying their thinking and consider what they might do and who they might tell and how if the response they received made them feel sad, upset or angry.

Your understanding in terms of contextual safeguarding is important here as you should avoid any situations that you know have caused particular distress to children.

SEXUAL ABUSE

This is an area that grabs the headlines. It is important to note that all genders and ages may be sexually abused, and victims are often scared to disclose as a result of guilt or fear. Males and females may commit sexual abuse as may other children. Awareness of this last fact is crucial if teachers are to avoid similar situations to one reported by the *Telegraph* in November 2018, where a 6 year-old girl was repeatedly sexually abused by boys in the playground. It is not just about the final act but includes *'forcing or enticing a child . . . to take part in sexual activities, not necessarily involving a high level of violence'* (DfE, 2018, p 14). Sexual abuse can involve contact and non-contact activities, such as children watching sexual activities, or grooming a child in preparation for abuse either in person or online. As with emotional abuse, this can be difficult to identify, and signs may be emotional or behavioural rather than physical.

NEGLECT

This is defined as *'the persistent failure to meet a child's basic physical and/or psychological needs, likely to result in the serious impairment of the child's health or development'* (DfE, 2018a, p 14). It may involve a parent or carer knowing about the physical or emotional danger faced by a child and doing nothing about it. Neglect can occur before a child is born, for example through maternal substance abuse. You should be alert to possible signs of neglect, for example, unclean or unsuitable clothing, a child's appearance, a child seeking food as they know school will be the only place they will be fed. In terms of appearance, sometimes there may be a medical diagnosis that accounts for a child's lack of development, known as organic failure to thrive. In cases where there is no medical diagnosis, known as non-organic failure to thrive, this can be an indicator of neglect.

Concerns

Safeguarding is a highly complex area, and there are often no clear-cut answers. In terms of best practice, you should clarify why you are concerned but always share your concerns with the safeguarding officer. Here are some useful prompts to support your thinking.

- What has made you concerned?
- What have you witnessed or observed?
- What have you heard through others?
- What has been said directly to you and by whom?

Record-keeping

You should be familiar with your school's system for recording safeguarding concerns. In any record-keeping, it is essential that you remain factual and avoid speculation, opinions or subjectivity. For example, 'the child was crying today' is a fact, whereas 'the child was sad today' is an opinion. All records should be written as soon as possible using the child's words as far as possible. Records need to remain confidential and be stored securely. You should identify the action taken and sign, including the date and time. Education uses a lot of jargon and acronyms; it is essential that you avoid these in any records and write with clarity to ensure accessibility for all audiences, which will involve people from a variety of professions.

Disclosures

Children may well disclose information to you, and this can be difficult to manage, but it is essential that you allow the child to speak without interruption or direct questioning. If a child says something that requires clarification, open questions are fine, but be mindful not to ask leading questions that could impede any future action. A child may ask you to keep what they tell you a secret. It is essential that you are clear with them that you cannot keep it a secret but do tell them who you will share it with, ie, the safeguarding officer, and the reason for this. Ongoing communication is also important so that the child knows what is happening. What you hear is likely to evoke an emotional response, but with the best interests of the child in mind it is important that you stay calm and avoid any obvious expression of shock. You should ensure active listening and not give your opinions. Reassurance is imperative so that children understand they have done the right thing by telling you. You may feel anxious about sharing information, but HM Government (2018, p 18) clearly states that, '*Fears about sharing information must not be allowed to stand in the way of the need to promote the welfare, and protect the safety, of children, which must always be the paramount concern.*'

Learning from past events

Over the years, there have been a number of serious case reviews following the deaths of children. These often highlight failings within the system, particularly in terms of inadequate information-sharing and alertness to signals. Such events have informed the legislation that you now have to abide by. The importance of everyone taking responsibility cannot be emphasised enough if we are to avoid cases like those raised through Serious Case Reviews happening again.

Child sexual exploitation

Child sexual exploitation (CSE) often makes the news and is a form of abuse through which children receive something for sexual activity. This involves coercion and sometimes may happen as a result of fear or desperation. There are a number of potential behavioural indicators that a child is a victim of CSE, including unexplained gifts, going missing, involvement with older people or known perpetrators, fear and criminal activity. Physical symptoms may also be evident in the form of injuries or self-harm. Alertness to potential signs is essential if you are to respond accordingly.

Peer-on-peer abuse

The DfE (2018b) has produced clear guidance on this issue. This emphasises that sexual violence and harassment are unacceptable and should not be part of growing up. Behaviour that may be criminal by definition must be challenged because dismissal or toleration of such behaviour can lead to it being deemed normal. This should be included as part of your school's behaviour and safeguarding policies.

Good practice example

DEVELOPING AN UNDERSTANDING OF WHAT IS APPROPRIATE AND INAPPROPRIATE CONDUCT

Using the National Society for the Prevention of Cruelty to Children (NSPCC) PANTS lesson plan (available at https://learning.nspcc.org.uk/media/1387/underwear-rule-resources-lesson-plan.pdf), develop the children's understanding of what is appropriate and inappropriate touching. This lesson will develop their confidence to say 'No' and enable them to identify who they can trust and who they may ask for help.

The link to the full range of PANTS materials can be found in the further reading and resources section of this chapter. Regularly refer to these issues and consider a display to reinforce key messages both in the classroom and around the school.

Honour-based abuse

This takes a range of forms and is based around defending the honour of families or communities.

FEMALE GENITAL MUTILATION

Female genital mutilation (FGM) has been a criminal offence in the UK since 1985, with the legislation being amended in 2003 to incorporate UK nationals or permanent UK residents taking their child abroad for the procedure. The first conviction for FGM in the UK occurred in early 2019. The procedure can take a number of forms, but the Crown Prosecution Service (2017) notes that *'The practice is medically unnecessary, is extremely painful and has serious health consequences, both at the time when the mutilation is carried out, and in later life.'* FGM can occur at any time during a child's life, but 5–8 year-olds are particularly at risk. You should be alert to children talking about going on a special holiday to the country from which their family originates or if they talk about an older female relative coming to stay. If, particularly after a longer school holiday, the child shows signs of physical discomfort or a change in behaviour, this could also be an indicator. As with other safeguarding concerns, you should follow school safeguarding procedures. With FGM, there is a mandatory reporting duty for teachers *'to report to the police where they discover (either through disclosure by the victim or visual evidence) that FGM appears to have been carried out on a girl under 18'* (DfE, 2018a, p 10).

FORCED MARRIAGE

It is important to note that a forced marriage is one that involves one or both people not consenting to the marriage. It is different to an arranged marriage, which involves consent from both parties with the option to refuse. In the UK, forced marriage is noted as a form of violence or abuse and is a serious breach of human rights. Education that reinforces strategies to say no and to recognise when something is not right in a relationship will go some way in supporting children's confidence and resilience in dealing with such issues in later life.

BREAST-IRONING

This involves the flattening of breasts through hard or heated objects in young girls, usually between the ages of 9 and 15. This is done to make the breasts disappear or to delay their development. It is considered that this protects girls from sexual contact or early forced marriage with a drive to keep them in education. At the moment there is no law specific to breast-ironing in the UK, but it is considered a form of physical abuse.

If you have any concerns about a child having been subject to or being at risk of honour-based abuse, you must follow usual child-protection procedures, noting the different approach in the case of FGM.

Children missing from education

Here you need to understand the procedures in terms of attendance monitoring, particularly in terms of unauthorised absence. The DfE (2018a) notes that repeated absence from school can suggest a range of potential safeguarding issues. You should follow your school's protocols to ensure early intervention to ensure the best outcomes for children.

Concerns about colleagues or procedures

Sadly, there may be times when you have concerns about the conduct of colleagues in your setting. Any concerns you have must be reported at the earliest opportunity to relevant senior leaders or governors. You should adhere to your school policy on this. It is not an easy or comfortable thing to do, but ultimately you need to be driven by the best interests of your pupils.

In terms of concerns about the robustness of safeguarding practices, these again must be raised so that appropriate action can be taken to ensure best outcomes for children. There are a range of whistleblowing procedures, both in school and beyond. If you have a concern, you have a duty to report it. Avoid the temptation to hope that someone else may have reported the issue; they probably will not have.

Summary

Safeguarding is about ensuring the best possible life chances for all children and is everyone's responsibility. It is an incredibly complex and multifaceted area. You need to maintain a mindset that recognises that abuse can happen anywhere. Children should have an active voice within safeguarding. You have a duty to record concerns in a clear, unambiguous and objective manner, sharing information with relevant parties, notably the safeguarding officer, to ensure that the complete picture is available as far as possible. Having a professional inquisitiveness will ensure that concerns are acted upon in the best interests of children. You are not alone and should always seek advice when you feel it is necessary.

Policy summary

POLICY	KEY POINTS	IMPLICATIONS FOR SCHOOLS
CHILDREN ACT (1989)	• PUT WELFARE OF CHILDREN AT THE CENTRE WHEN MAKING DECISIONS. • INTRODUCED THE CONCEPT OF PARENTAL RESPONSIBILITY. • ENABLED CHILDREN TO BE INVOLVED IN LEGAL PROCEEDINGS.	• ENSURE THAT CHILDREN'S WELFARE IS AT THE CENTRE OF ALL OF YOUR WORK.

POLICY	KEY POINTS	IMPLICATIONS FOR SCHOOLS
	· GAVE LOCAL AUTHORITIES A DUTY TO IDENTIFY AND SAFEGUARD CHILDREN'S WELFARE WHERE THEY WERE IDENTIFIED AS BEING IN NEED. · INTRODUCED THE CONCEPT OF SIGNIFICANT HARM TO WARRANT COMPULSORY INTERVENTION IN FAMILY LIFE.	· ENSURE THAT YOU FOLLOW CORRECT PROTOCOLS WHEN DEALING WITH CHILDREN'S DISCLOSURES; AVOID LEADING QUESTIONS WHICH COULD MEAN THAT THEIR EVIDENCE IS NOT ADMISSIBLE IN COURT; KEEP CLEAR, OBJECTIVE RECORDS IN ACCORDANCE WITH SCHOOL PROCEDURE; AND SEEK ADVICE WHERE NECESSARY FROM YOUR SAFEGUARDING OFFICER. · WHERE YOU HAVE REASONABLE CAUSE TO BELIEVE THAT A CHILD MAY BE SUFFERING OR IS LIKELY TO SUFFER SIGNIFICANT HARM, YOU SHOULD MAKE A REFERRAL.
CHILDREN ACT (2004)	· EMPHASISED INDIVIDUAL AND CORPORATE RESPONSIBILITY TO PROMOTE CHILDREN'S WELFARE. · PROMOTED MORE COORDINATED AND EFFECTIVE INFORMATION-SHARING AND PARTNERSHIP WORKING.	· ENGAGE WITH RELEVANT PARTNERS IN ORDER TO CONTRIBUTE TO THE BROADER PICTURE FOR ANY INDIVIDUAL CHILD.
CHILD AND SOCIAL WORK ACT (2017)	· IMPROVED SUPPORT FOR LOOKED AFTER AND PREVIOUSLY LOOKED AFTER CHILDREN. · PROMOTED PARTNERSHIP WORKING LOCALLY TO IMPROVE CHILD-PROTECTION PRACTICE. · PROMOTED SAFEGUARDING BY PROVIDING RELATIONSHIPS AND SEX EDUCATION IN SCHOOLS.	· BE AWARE OF ISSUES AROUND THOSE CHILDREN WHO ARE EITHER LOOKED AFTER OR HAVE BEEN PREVIOUSLY LOOKED AFTER. · DEVELOP GOOD-QUALITY PROVISION IN TERMS OF RELATIONSHIPS (AND SEX) EDUCATION.

POLICY	KEY POINTS	IMPLICATIONS FOR SCHOOLS
EDUCATION ACT (2002)	· INTRODUCED THE DUTY TO SAFEGUARD AND PROMOTE CHILDREN'S WELFARE IN EDUCATION SETTINGS.	· THERE SHOULD BE AN APPROPRIATELY TRAINED TEACHER WHO OVERSEES AND PROMOTES EDUCATIONAL ACHIEVEMENT FOR CHILDREN WHO ARE LOOKED AFTER/PREVIOUSLY LOOKED AFTER. · ENSURE COMPLIANCE WITH SAFER RECRUITMENT PROCESSES AND VIGILANCE. · ANNUAL TRAINING AND REGULAR UPDATES ARE PARTICULARLY IMPORTANT FACTORS IN ACHIEVING THIS.
WORKING TOGETHER TO SAFEGUARD CHILDREN (2018)	· NOTES HOW INDIVIDUALS AND ORGANISATIONS SHOULD WORK TOGETHER TO SAFEGUARD AND PROMOTE CHILDREN'S WELFARE. · REFLECTS CURRENT LEGISLATION, POLICY AND PRACTICE.	· UNDERSTAND YOUR RESPONSIBILITIES IN RELATION TO THIS DOCUMENT.
LOCAL SAFEGUARDING CHILDREN BOARDS (LSCBs)	· SET OUT THE PROCEDURES AND POLICIES FOR YOU TO FOLLOW IN YOUR SETTING. · IDENTIFY CURRENT SAFEGUARDING PRIORITIES IN YOUR LOCAL AREA.	· UNDERSTAND THE POLICIES AND PROCEDURES SET OUT BY THE LCSB RELEVANT TO YOUR SETTING. · ACCESS INFORMATION FROM THE LCSB WEBSITE AS THIS WILL ENSURE YOU ARE ACCESSING THE MOST CURRENT INFORMATION. IT DOES CHANGE REGULARLY, SO AVOID PRINTING MATERIALS AS THEY WILL SOON BE OUT OF DATE.
KEEPING CHILDREN SAFE IN EDUCATION (2018)	· STATUTORY GUIDANCE FOR ALL SCHOOLS.	· YOU MUST BE FAMILIAR WITH THIS GUIDANCE AND HAVE READ AT LEAST PART ONE OF THE DOCUMENT. YOUR SCHOOL WILL ASK YOU TO SIGN TO CONFIRM THAT YOU HAVE READ AND UNDERSTOOD THIS.

POLICY	KEY POINTS	IMPLICATIONS FOR SCHOOLS
		· ANNEX A IS ALSO USEFUL IN PROVIDING GREATER DETAIL ABOUT KEY ISSUES THAT WILL AFFECT YOUR ROLE.
SCHOOL SAFEGUARDING POLICY AND PROCEDURES	· TAILORED TO YOUR SETTING BASED ON THE NATIONAL STATUTORY GUIDANCE.	· ENSURE FULL UNDERSTANDING AND ADHERENCE TO SCHOOL POLICY AND PROCEDURES AT ALL TIMES.
SEXUAL VIOLENCE AND SEXUAL HARASSMENT BETWEEN CHILDREN IN SCHOOLS AND COLLEGES (DFE GUIDANCE, MAY 2018)	· THIS, ALONGSIDE *KEEPING CHILDREN SAFE IN EDUCATION*, PROVIDES ADVICE FOR SCHOOLS ABOUT SEXUAL VIOLENCE AND HARASSMENT, RELATING TO CHILDREN OF ALL AGES. IT PROVIDES CLEAR DEFINITIONS AND IDENTIFIES WHAT SCHOOLS NEED TO BE ALERT TO. IT ALSO SIGNPOSTS LINKS TO OTHER RELEVANT DOCUMENTATION.	· UNDERSTAND THE ISSUES TO BE ALERT TO, ALONGSIDE YOUR STATUTORY DUTIES IN TERMS OF ADDRESSING INCIDENTS OF PEER-ON-PEER ABUSE.
MANDATORY REPORTING OF FGM: PROCEDURAL INFORMATION (HOME OFFICE, 2015)	· OUTLINES REQUIREMENTS FOR RELEVANT PROFESSIONALS.	· ENSURE FULL UNDERSTANDING AND COMPLIANCE WITH THE MANDATORY REPORTING DUTY.

POLICY	KEY POINTS	IMPLICATIONS FOR SCHOOLS
OFSTED SCHOOL INSPECTION HANDBOOK (2018)	· SAFEGUARDING IS A KEY FOCUS FOR OFSTED. THE GRADING CRITERIA STATES: – OUTSTANDING: SAFEGUARDING IS EFFECTIVE. LEADERS AND MANAGERS HAVE CREATED A CULTURE OF VIGILANCE WHERE PUPILS' WELFARE IS ACTIVELY PROMOTED. PUPILS ARE LISTENED TO AND FEEL SAFE. STAFF ARE TRAINED TO IDENTIFY WHEN A PUPIL MAY BE AT RISK OF NEGLECT, ABUSE OR EXPLOITATION AND THEY REPORT THEIR CONCERNS. LEADERS AND STAFF WORK EFFECTIVELY WITH EXTERNAL PARTNERS TO SUPPORT PUPILS WHO ARE AT RISK OR WHO ARE THE SUBJECT OF A MULTI-AGENCY PLAN. – GOOD: SAFEGUARDING IS EFFECTIVE. LEADERS AND STAFF TAKE APPROPRIATE ACTION TO IDENTIFY PUPILS WHO MAY BE AT RISK OF NEGLECT, ABUSE OR SEXUAL EXPLOITATION, REPORTING CONCERNS AND SUPPORTING THE NEEDS OF THOSE PUPILS. – RI (REQUIRES IMPROVEMENT): SAFEGUARDING IS EFFECTIVE.	· CONSIDER YOUR SCHOOL'S PRACTICE IN RELATION TO THIS CRITERIA AND THE EVIDENCE YOU HAVE TO SUPPORT YOUR CLAIMS. IDENTIFY WHERE ACTION IS NEEDED TO ENHANCE PRACTICE.

POLICY	KEY POINTS	IMPLICATIONS FOR SCHOOLS
	- INADEQUATE: SAFEGUARDING IS INEFFECTIVE. THE SCHOOL'S ARRANGEMENTS FOR SAFEGUARDING PUPILS DO NOT MEET STATUTORY REQUIREMENTS, OR THEY GIVE SERIOUS CAUSE FOR CONCERN OR INSUFFICIENT ACTION IS TAKEN TO REMEDY WEAKNESSES FOLLOWING A SERIOUS INCIDENT.	

❖ Critical questions

1. Are you up to date in terms of your mandatory safeguarding training?

2. What have you done to remain up to date with the most recent developments? What will you do now as a result of reading this chapter?

3. How has your engagement with training and updates impacted upon your practice and outcomes for children?

4. How effectively do you communicate with relevant colleagues about safeguarding concerns?

5. How well do you understand the broader picture and background for the children you teach? What might you do to enhance this?

6. Have you read anything in this chapter that you were not aware of? What will you do as a result of this?

7. How confident do you feel in terms of distinguishing between fact and opinion when recording your concerns?

8. How clearly do you record concerns to ensure accessibility for relevant parties, avoiding profession-specific jargon and acronyms?

9. Which resources will you integrate into your teaching and how will you share these with parents? What impact do you intend to have by using these resources?

further reading and resources

HM Government (March 2015) What to Do If You're Worried a Child Is Being Abused: Advice for Practitioners	Non-statutory guidance to support you in making decisions if you are concerned a child is being abused.
HM Government (July 2018) Information Sharing: Advice for Practitioners Providing Safeguarding Services to Children, Young People, Parents and Carers	This provides clear guidance on best practice regarding information sharing.
DfE advice on whistleblowing (www. gov.uk/guidance/whistleblowing-procedure-for-maintained-schools)	Guidance on setting up a whistleblowing policy in school.
NSPCC Whistleblowing advice line (www.nspcc.org.uk/what-you-can-do/report-abuse/dedicated-helplines/whistleblowing-advice-line)	This gives guidance and support if you have concerns about policy and practice in your setting.
NSPCC CASPAR update service (https://learning.nspcc.org.uk/newsletter/caspar)	Sign up to this to receive weekly updates about developments related to practice, policy and research related to safeguarding and child protection.
Safeguarding in schools website (Andrew Hall) (www. safeguardinginschools.co.uk/andrew-hall)	A range of information related to the latest developments and current policy and practice related to safeguarding. Scroll down to the bottom of the homepage to sign up for email updates.
Schools Improvement (https://schoolsimprovement.net)	A website containing a digest of all education news. You can search for key words, including related to safeguarding issues.
National FGM Centre Resources (http://nationalfgmcentre.org.uk/fgm/fgm-direct-work-toolkit)	Resources to support teachers' work about FGM with children from the age of 7 and parents/carers.
NSPCC Preventing Abuse (www.nspcc.org.uk/preventing-abuse)	A website containing a range of helpful information that will support you in keeping children safe.
Refuge domestic violence(www. refuge.org.uk)	A comprehensive website which explores issues around domestic violence for women and children. There is some useful information about the effects of domestic violence on children.

UNICEF Behind Closed Doors (www.unicef.org/media/files/ BehindClosedDoors.pdf)	A document which explores the impact of domestic violence on children.
NSPCC Domestic Abuse (www.nspcc. org.uk/preventing-abuse/child-abuse-and-neglect/domestic-abuse)	Explores what domestic abuse is and its impact on children.
Women's Aid, the Impact of Domestic Abuse on Children and Young People (www.womensaid.org.uk/information-support/what-is-domestic-abuse/ impact-on-children-and-young-people)	Identifies how domestic abuse may impact on children and young people.
Young Minds (https://youngminds. org.uk/find-help/for-parents/parents-guide-to-support-a-z/parents-guide-to-support-domestic-violence)	Guidance on how to support children who have witnessed or experienced domestic violence.
The Children's Society, Domestic Abuse (www.childrenssociety.org. uk/substance-misuse-domestic-violence/domestic-violence/ what-is-domestic-violence)	Explores the concept of domestic abuse and how young people who have been affected may be supported.
Childline, Domestic Abuse (www. childline.org.uk/info-advice/home-families/family-relationships/ domestic-abuse)	Guidance on what domestic abuse is and what can be done about it.
Barnardo's, Domestic Violence (www. barnardos.org.uk/what_we_do/our_ projects/domestic_violence.htm)	Information and advice concerning domestic abuse and children.
NHS, information about FGM (www.nhs.uk/conditions/ female-genital-mutilation-fgm)	Information about FGM, including awareness raising material.
NSPCC, information about FGM (www.nspcc.org.uk/preventing-abuse/child-abuse-and-neglect/ female-genital-mutilation-fgm)	Contains a range of information about FGM, including signs, indicators and effects as well as guidance about how to prevent this happening to protect potential victims.
Childline, information about FGM (www.childline.org.uk/info-advice/ bullying-abuse-safety/abuse-safety/ female-circumcision-fgm-cutting)	A range of information about FGM, including sources of help.

Home Office FGM resource pack (www.gov.uk/government/ publications/female-genital- mutilation-resource-pack/female- genital-mutilation-resource-pack)	This offers suggestions of good practice and provides clarity about professional responsibilities related to FGM.
National FGM Centre, FGM resources (http://nationalfgmcentre.org.uk/ fgm/fgm-resources)	A wide range of resources, including for education that will help you to fulfil your responsibilities and engage fully with the issues.
NSPCC CSE (www.nspcc.org.uk/ preventing-abuse/child-abuse-and- neglect/child-sexual-exploitation)	A range of information and resources to support education and care for children in terms of CSE.
Barnardo's CSE (www.barnardos.org. uk/what_we_do/our_work/sexual_ exploitation.htm)	A range of resources to support understanding of issues around CSE.
GOV.UK, Forced marriage guidance (www.gov.uk/guidance/ forced-marriage)	Guidance about protecting, advising and supporting victims of forced marriage.
National Children's Bureau, Children missing education (www.ncb.org.uk/ resources-publications/resources/ children-missing-education)	A report about children missing education and its impact.
GOV.UK statutory guidance on children missing education (www. gov.uk/government/publications/ children-missing-education)	Statutory guidance on how to help children missing education back into it.
NHS Fabricated or induced illness information (www.nhs.uk/conditions/ fabricated-or-induced-illness)	Information about fabricated or induced illness, including signs, causes and what to do as a professional.
TES/NSPCC article about the role of schools in relation to fabricated or induced illness (www.tes.com/ teaching-resource/fabricated- induced-illness-the-role-of-schools- 6435151)	This article identifies the role of schools in response to concerns about fabricated or induced illness in children.

GOV.UK, Safeguarding Children in Whom Illness Is Fabricated or Induced (www.gov.uk/government/publications/safeguarding-children-in-whom-illness-is-fabricated-or-induced)	Statutory guidance which identifies what schools should do in cases of fabricated or induced illness in order to comply with the law.
DfE National Action Plan to Tackle Child Abuse Linked to Faith or Belief (https://assets.publishing.service.gov.uk/government/uploads/system/uploads/attachment_data/file/175437/Action_Plan_-_Abuse_linked_to_Faith_or_Belief.pdf)	Guidance for anyone working with children about how to prevent child abuse stemming from religion or superstition.
NSPCC PANTS resources (www.nspcc.org.uk/preventing-abuse/keeping-children-safe/underwear-rule)	A range of child-friendly resources which engage children with strategies to keep them safe from abuse.

References

Crown Prosecution Service (2017) Female Genital Mutilation Prosecution Guidance. [online] Available at: www.cps.gov.uk/legal-guidance/female-genital-mutilation-prosecution-guidance (accessed 4 January 2019).

Department for Education (2018a) *Keeping Children Safe in Education*. London: DfE.

Department for Education (2018b) *Sexual Violence and Sexual Harassment Between Children in Schools and Colleges*. London: DfE.

Hardy, J (2018) First Ever Payout for Primary School Sex Assault After Girl, 6, Was Repeatedly Abused by Boys in the Playground. [online] Available at: www.telegraph.co.uk/news/2018/11/21/first-ever-payout-primary-school-sex-assault-girl-6-repeatedly/ (accessed 4 January 2019).

HM Government (2018) Working Together to Safeguard Children. [online] Available at: https://assets.publishing.service.gov.uk/government/uploads/system/uploads/attachment_data/file/729914/Working_Together_to_Safeguard_Children-2018.pdf (accessed 4 January 2019).

3. ONLINE SAFETY: IT'S A JUNGLE OUT THERE!

Key issues

Technology and online devices play an increasingly significant part in children's lives and, while bringing numerous benefits, pose the potential for significant risk to all aspects of their well-being. Childnet (2018) provides a range of statistics about child ownership and use of online devices. Two statistics that particularly stand out are that 79 per cent of 5–7 year-olds spend around nine hours per week online; 63 per cent of these largely use a tablet to go online. With significant figures such as these, your duty as a teacher to support children and their parents in navigating these tricky and ever-evolving waters is paramount.

There continue to be rapid developments in technology, growing rates of cybercrime and regular reports in the media about how people's gullibility online is causing significant issues. Technological advances are challenging, ever-evolving and complex. When I was at school, the latest trends were visible, with yo-yos being in vogue one week and stretchy rubber figures the next. Now, technology forms the basis of current trends, and you need to maintain an astute awareness of these so that potential issues can be addressed in a timely fashion, such as those seen with the game Fortnite. With over half of 5–7 year-olds accessing such activity on portable devices, keeping track of their pastimes is problematic.

What do children do online?

This is difficult to answer, but, at a basic level, they will be using the internet to:

- search for information;
- share images;
- watch videos;
- engage with social media;
- engage with message boards and discussion forums;
- play games (alone or with others, physically or virtually);
- chat with others through online games.

It is easy to make assumptions about what children will be doing online, based on our own experiences, but you need to engage with resources such as NSPCC Net Aware, which identifies the range of online resources that children may be using. Your proactive research and engagement are important so you can understand the range of resources available, how these may be of benefit as well as how they may be potentially dangerous. While you may not engage directly with applications such as Snapchat, it is important that you at least have an understanding about functionality. Ofcom (2017) research about media use and attitudes found that Snapchat has overtaken Facebook and WhatsApp in terms of popularity with children. Without a level of working knowledge and understanding of these applications you will be restricted in terms of the support you can provide. Ofcom (2017, p 12) notes that, '*"Snapstreaks", when two people on Snapchat send an image to each other every day over consecutive days, is particularly popular, and many of the children were maintaining streaks even with children they were not friends with.*'

- Do you know how Snapchat works?
- Did you know what a Snapstreak was?

These are the types of questions you need to be routinely considering as part of your ongoing awareness of current trends so that you comprehend what children are using and how as well as considering the types of pressures such applications may put on children.

The NSPCC Net Aware report (2017a) noted the following opportunities provided by the internet from young people's perspectives:

- fun;
- communication;
- self-expression;
- creativity;
- privacy settings (while provision of these by sites was a strength, it was noted that knowledge of such settings is variable).

Issues around online safety hit the headlines and feature as major storylines in popular culture, such as in soaps, and you must acknowledge these storylines with children in an attempt to support them in making sense of the issues that arise. This is not to scare children but to equip them for life in a digital world in a bid to empower them to take ownership for their own safety online. The dangers that you need to acknowledge and facilitate open, honest discussions around include:

- inappropriate content, including pornography;
- the ignoring of age restrictions;
- friending/communicating with strangers;
- grooming, sexual abuse;
- sharing of personal information (often because the default setting on applications is insecure; allowing for the indiscriminate and unwitting sharing of personal data);
- gambling or running up debt.

Social media

Social media, while having many advantages that can serve to boost well-being, such as reconnecting with an old friend or enabling social interaction, can be an incredibly divisive and damaging tool. Most people feel the need to be popular, and this can cause issues with young people in terms of who is a real friend and who is a virtual friend. In 2017, *The Guardian* reported on a study that showed that the more time children spent on social media the less happy they were in most elements of their life.

It is all too easy to share virtually anything through social media, so you need to engage children with taking responsibility for the personal information they share. The use of real-life contexts and analogies is useful here. For example, would the children produce an A4 paper giving information about themselves, location, school, friends and hobbies and then print 500 copies to be handed out to complete strangers on the local high street? Generally, the answer here will be no, but without such analogies, children's understanding of the real-world equivalent of digital footprints will be limited.

SOCIAL MEDIA: ITS POTENTIAL IMPACT ON BODY IMAGE AND MENTAL HEALTH

Evidence from the Department of Health and Social Care (DHSC, 2018), '*shows that children who spend more than 3 hours using social networking websites on a school day are twice as likely to report high or very high scores for mental ill health.*' The Safer Internet Centre (2018) talks about the concept of '*digital well-being*' and how you need to engage children with considering the impact of online activity on their holistic well-being (physical, emotional and mental). With continual developments in technology, children need to be equipped with the skills to regulate and recognise these issues with a level of independence. Work in this area is ongoing and is an area of high priority for the DHSC and the chief medical officer.

With images being a key way to communicate via social media, there is a concern about the impact on body image, in particular with applications that enable the editing of photographs to enhance the subject's appearance. It is not just the act of sharing an edited photograph; the response of others can have a significant impact. This negative impact could result from a number of factors, including a low number of likes or positive comments and nasty comments which are anonymised as well as delayed or non-instant responses from peers. In light of this, you need to implement a range of routine approaches which will develop children's resilience and give them the confidence to understand that not everyone in life will like them and that this is OK.

Parental online behaviour

When addressing online safety, parents are a crucial element. There are issues concerning their appropriate behaviour online which should be encouraged so that they can provide a positive model of behaviour to their children. 'Sharenting' refers to parents sharing photographs of their children on social media, which can pose dangers, including fraud. The BBC (2018) reported that disclosure of personal details such as name, age, birthday, pets' names, sports teams and the like has the potential to give information (that is permanently available once posted) that could be used to hack passwords and forge identity. Barclays Bank (BBC, 2018) estimates that, '*parents over-sharing information online will produce 7.4 million incidents per year of identity fraud by 2030.*' With this in mind, you play a key role in the education of parents related to the very real dangers of what may be routine online behaviour.

Figures from Ofcom show that there are significant numbers of children who could potentially be in danger of some form of harm, whether this be physical, economic, social or emotional, due to the behaviours of their parents. Parents who share photos may often do this without the permission of their children and may share without considering who may be able to access the material. This is an important point for you to raise, perhaps through parent workshops. It is important that children understand the importance of asking for permission before posting material online, but if their parents do not seek this, children will need to be supported in developing their understanding here. This issue also needs to be addressed through the model you provide as a teacher; each time you take a photo, ask permission to take and share the photo and engage children in what may happen to that image once it has been shared online. This should include discussion about what may be said about the photograph in an attempt to anticipate potential reactions to an image and enhance children's resilience to cope with negative comments.

SUPPORTING PARENTAL ENGAGEMENT

Access is always an issue in terms of work with parents and while workshops involving children working alongside their parents, teachers and peers are most desirable, this will not always be possible. Organisations, such as Childnet International and the UK Safer Internet Centre have produced comprehensive guidance about the potential impact of online resources on children's lives. The Ealing Grid for Learning hosts an online safety toolkit for parents which links to a broad range of relevant issues. These resources could be used to engage parents in meaningful conversations about a variety of online safety issues as it is important for children to explore sites together with their parents to celebrate the positive elements and to consider how to address areas for concern or caution. This structured discussion will facilitate the reasoning and rationalisation of thoughts.

THE IMPORTANCE OF TALK

The potential disconnect between teachers, parents and their children in relation to online savviness, can lead to hiding or fear, particularly when children come across something online (often accidentally) that makes them feel uncomfortable. The reality is that children will come across inappropriate, upsetting material, but they need to develop a confident language to share their concerns. The Net Aware and Share Aware resources on the NSPCC website provide helpful information to support informed teacher and parental discussions with children about online behaviour and safety. These discussions will be most meaningful when they relate to the resources that children are actually using at the moment. Children and their parents need to explore sites and applications together with a focus on balanced evaluation in order to empower children to deal with areas of concern. The talk should be positive in nature and facilitate discussion about things children have seen that make them feel uncomfortable. Smoothwall (2018) reports that in cases of online abuse, 37 per cent of children will talk to no one, 25 per cent will talk to a parent or carer and 5 per cent will talk to a teacher, showing that significant work needs to be done to build confidence to ensure regular dialogue.

All sites and applications should have a reporting function, but often children and those supporting them do not know where these functions are or how to use them. As part of your teaching you need to engage children, regularly, with issues around how to block inappropriate contact or content and how to keep their personal information private in that context. A basic but effective way to do this is avoiding obvious usernames or passwords. Children from a young age are sharing images. Here, the model provided by adults will impact on children's behaviour, but you need to structure discussions around the type of image they share and the message (intentional or unintentional) that this may give to someone who can access it.

Some useful questions to include as part of your discussions are:

- What do you enjoy doing online? Which app is your favourite?
- What is good about the app?
- What makes you feel sad or angry when using the app?
- Have any issues arisen and what are they?
- How might these issues be overcome?

- Who can you talk to who can help keep you safe?
- Where are the reporting functions?
- Do you know how to use the reporting functions?
- How do you block someone?
- How are you keeping personal information private?

Legal issues

The issue of sexting frequently hits the headlines. This refers to the sending of explicit images or messages via online devices. There are key legal issues here that children need to be educated about from an early age so that they do not unwittingly fall foul of the legal system. The law states that it is illegal to create, send or store indecent photographs of anyone under the age of 18. Children absolutely need to understand this, including what to do in terms of reporting if they receive an image. Failure to report could lead to them being seen to be in possession of an indecent image of a minor; a criminal offence. The importance of open discussion is pivotal here. In terms of developing resilience, you need to teach children about how to deal with possible coercion to send such images through discussion and use of reporting and blocking functions.

GENERAL DATA PROTECTION REGULATION

Since May 2018, the General Data Protection Regulation (GDPR) has been law, replacing the 1998 Data Protection Act. This is about ensuring transparency about the data held by an organisation. Privacy notices are the mechanism by which this information is conveyed, and schools should update their policies at appropriate intervals to ensure that pupil data is used by the school in a fair and transparent manner. This also has implications in terms of the storage of data. You need to ensure full compliance with your school's policies about data handling to ensure the avoidance of a data breach. One example of this is the use of cloud-based storage to eliminate the need for USB memory sticks, though if memory sticks are used they should be encrypted and password protected. This modelling of best practice should be embedded throughout your teaching in terms of ensuring security of information.

The Byron Review

The issue of online safety has been a cause for concern for many years. In 2008, Professor Tanya Byron was commissioned to conduct a comprehensive review of online safety, particularly regarding the internet and video games. From this, guidelines were generated with a focus on the opportunities and risks provided by online resources. A number of opportunities were identified, which mirror those discussed earlier in this chapter. Risks related to commercial elements (advertising and spam), aggressive and hateful content, sexual risk, including access to pornography, meeting strangers and being groomed as well as creating and uploading indecent material. Values in terms of biased information and advice were also highlighted as areas of risk.

Byron's work, in addition to considering opportunities and risks, classified risk based on the following:

- Content: children are recipients through being exposed to illegal, inappropriate or harmful material.
- Contact: children are participants through being subjected to harmful online interaction with others.
- Conduct: children are actors, in that their personal behaviour in an online environment increases the likelihood of, or causes, harm.

These should encourage you to think about children not just as potential victims of online activity but also how they may be involved in the harm produced. This has clearly fed into the current UK curriculum requirements (DfE, 2013) which focus on children being respectful and responsible users.

In 2018, a ten-year progress report was published by the NSPCC, which reinforces the need for swift action, particularly in light of the speed at which the online world continues to develop and evolve. The NSPCC (2017b) notes that only thirteen out of the thirty-eight recommendations have been fully implemented, and there are calls for further action. Pages 17–22 of the document highlight what has been achieved to date and where further work is needed. You should consider how you can support progress towards the achievement of these targets.

Cyberbullying

We used to talk about stranger danger in the context of an outside environment. With such rapid development of portable, wireless technology, strangers can be in the child's bedroom and alongside them at all times. This is not to say that it is just strangers who pose the danger to children. Cyberbullying will often be done by those known to an individual. Of course, bullying is nothing new, but the nature of bullying continues to evolve into a potentially all-consuming force. Lasher and Baker (2015) note in their study how there are actually fewer 'school bullies' now, but that cyberbullying is on the increase. You need to understand the issue of cyberbullying and be proactive in recognising when this is happening through alertness to signs and also active monitoring of online systems in school.

Cyberbullying may present itself in a range of forms, including:

- the use of technology to deliberately cause upset, humiliation or threat;
- unpleasant online communication;
- abusive online messages;
- posting of humiliating images or videos;
- spreading rumours;

- prank calls or messages;
- establishing or contributing to a hate site.

This can happen in a range of contexts, including mobile phones, websites, forums, social media or gaming systems. It is easier for bullies to hide behind an anonymous identity online or to pretend to be someone else behind their screen. Related to this, Phippen (2018) makes the following point, '*we need to develop critical thinking and digital literacy that goes beyond whether content is "good" or "bad" and explore how it makes people feel and how we might counteract how upset is caused.*'

Education and regular focus on respectful and responsible use of technology is part of the solution to embed this message. Children need to be supported in their consideration not just about their actions but the potentially devastating consequences their actions may have on a recipient. As children may use a range of media for cyberbullying activity, it is essential that you remain up to date with trends and applications so that you can effectively engage children and educate appropriately to reduce instances of cyberbullying as much as possible.

ENSURING RELEVANCE TO LEARNERS

In terms of education, you need to consider what is needed and most appropriate based on the needs and experiences of your learners at any given time; this has potential to change regularly. Children will also see storylines in popular culture unfolding about this issue, and you need to reflect upon how you may incorporate some of these storylines into your teaching so that children have a safe, structured environment in which they can make sense of what they are seeing.

PARENTS AND CYBERBULLYING

There is a need to engage parents with the issue so that they can be alert to the potential signals of cyberbullying. The DfE, in addition to their *Preventing and Tackling Bullying* (2017) document, provide supplementary advice for heads and teachers as well as for parents and carers. There is a danger that children will be embarrassed by the online harassment they are receiving and may not speak to an adult about this. Parents should be made aware that some children use acronyms such as PIL (parent in room) to hide their activity, and how this could be a cause for concern if not swiftly addressed.

Safer school systems

The growth of the internet means that filters are not as secure as we would want them to be to keep children safe from a range of potentially harmful and upsetting material. This causes an issue in terms of how you use the internet with children in school. Paragraph 84 of *Keeping Children Safe in Education* (DfE, 2018, p 22) states the need for '*appropriate filters and monitoring systems*' to be in place in schools. This is further clarified by stating, '*they should be careful that "over blocking" does not lead to unreasonable restrictions as to what children can be taught with regards to online teaching and safeguarding.'* This has its dangers as children may come across inappropriate material because the version of the internet children are accessing is not the highly sanitised version that some may want for their children. Having said this, it does provide them with a realistic experience of the internet, as they will have at home and in everyday life. Phippen (2018) states, *'We need to move beyond "online safety" to better understand how we may develop resilience in young people, so they can deal with what they see and do online, rather than just hoping they avoid it completely.'*

The key point here is that issues around talk, reporting and blocking must be embedded into everyday teaching and learning activity involving the internet. Benefits stemming from this are that children will be given a real context for applying their understanding of how to keep themselves safe online. This should lead to reduced levels of vulnerability as they will be empowered to independently assess and manage the risks with which they are presented. There is a need to balance risks with the need to inform and educate children to prepare them for the real world. This approach needs to be understood and applied by all parties in school to ensure consistency and efficacy of the approach.

Despite monitored systems being a requirement since 2016, there is concern about how well schools are monitoring usage of online resources. Monitored systems should enable schools to identify potential cases of cyberbullying and report on this, but training is needed to ensure effective use of such systems. This is a key part of a school's safeguarding duty, and, at the moment, the data suggests that many cases are going unnoticed.

ACCEPTABLE-USE POLICIES

Acceptable-use policies (AUPs) are essential documents to ensure understanding and compliance of online usage within any educational setting. These should be live documents which are embedded into daily practice and revised regularly to reflect developments in technology or changing trends in use. They should be adapted to various user groups including staff, pupils (different for various age phases), parents, governors and visitors. In addition to adapted versions for various users, an AUP should be tailored to your particular setting to take account of the context. It is essential that the relevant policy is shared with, and signed by, everyone to show their understanding and acceptance of the rules. It is not sufficient to just have the policy, albeit up to date: the children must be fully conversant with the rules for internet usage and understand the risks associated with various types of online behaviour, including posting content on the internet.

Any AUP must be written in accessible language. It should talk about:

- keeping passwords and personal data private;
- only working with people the children know in real life and never agreeing to meet a stranger;
- courteous and respectful communication;
- showing and talking to an adult if something makes them feel upset;

- the Child Exploitation and Online Protection (CEOP) button and when/how to use it;
- the fact that anything an individual does on a computer may be seen by someone else (digital footprint).

Good practice example

AUPS

Provide regular (termly) opportunities for children to review their AUP to celebrate successes but also to identify any issues. Engage the children in discussing how these issues may be overcome and empower them to amend the policy. This will ensure that this is a live document and that children have true ownership of it. Exploit any opportunity for children to contribute to such policies so that you are assured the policy is relevant to their current experiences and use of technology based on current trends.

Good practice example

USE OF REAL-LIFE ANALOGIES

The idea of a digital survival kit (a good example can be found at https://edtechdigest. com/2013/10/18/digital-survival) is to help children associate items in the real world with their online equivalent. This web link gives a range of examples and it is useful to give children one idea as a starter but then let them generate their own. This will support them in understanding the importance of key aspects of the AUP, for example, a toothbrush as a metaphor for a password. You would not share your toothbrush with other people, nor would you want other people using your toothbrush. You will be amazed with the creative analogies that children devise!

The curriculum

Online safety has been a key issue in the UK curriculum for many years and is reflected in the national curriculum for computing (DfE, 2013), with emphasis on safe and respectful use, privacy of information and understanding how to seek help if children have concerns. As part of these requirements, it is essential that you engage in regular conversation with children about their online activity and habits to ensure that your work around online safety is relevant to their experience in order to have a positive impact. This is particularly important as these trends will spread very quickly amongst peers. While knowing about the technologies children use, it is also important for you to understand the functionality of these applications, even if you do not use them personally. The NSPCC resources provide a solid starting point for your research into these. It is also important that your teaching highlights issues around privacy settings and digital footprints so that children develop a working understanding and continual awareness of issues that will impact on any online activity. *Keeping Children Safe in Education* (DfE, 2018) talks about the importance of online safety issues being embedded throughout a broad and balanced curriculum not just in computing lessons as this will ensure a greater breadth, depth and application of learning.

Preparing children for the digital age

In light of the growing concerns highlighted throughout this chapter and emphasised by the NSPCC (2017a), including the current level of risk online for children being unacceptable, the need for the government and social-media companies to have greater responsibility for ensuring the necessary safeguards are in place instead of young people having to protect themselves and the need for young people to be actively involved in any decision-making as we move forward, there is much work going on. The *Growing Up Digital* report (Children's Commissioner for England, 2017) called for:

- the creation of a digital citizenship programme that should be compulsory in every school from age 4 to 14;
- the implementation of the GDPR from 2018;
- a new children's digital ombudsman to mediate between under 18s and social-media companies.

Almost alongside this, HM Government (2017) produced an *Internet Safety Strategy* green paper with the aim of addressing online safety in a joined-up manner by synthesising groups. This is driven by three key principles.

1. What is unacceptable in the real world should be unacceptable in the virtual world.

2. All users should be empowered to manage online risks and stay safe.

3. Technology companies should be responsible to their users.

There is clearly much more to do in regard to online safety, but it is important that you build on the work that has been done to date and truly embed these principles in your practice. Throughout the curriculum, consider how you model, embed and engage in relation to online safety and digital literacy.

Policy summary

POLICY	KEY POINTS	IMPLICATIONS FOR SCHOOLS
KEEPING CHILDREN SAFE IN EDUCATION (DFE, 2018)	· ALL STAFF MUST UNDERGO SAFEGUARDING AND CHILD-PROTECTION TRAINING AT INDUCTION (INCLUDING ONLINE SAFETY). THIS SHOULD BE RENEWED ANNUALLY, AND STAFF SHOULD TAKE RESPONSIBILITY FOR KEEPING UP TO DATE. · PART 5 REFERS TO CHILD-ON-CHILD SEXUAL VIOLENCE AND HARASSMENT WHICH MAY OCCUR ONLINE AND OFFLINE. · ONLINE SAFETY IS A KEY RESPONSIBILITY OF THE DESIGNATED SAFEGUARDING LEAD. · SUPPORTING MATERIALS RELATED TO ONLINE SAFETY ARE AVAILABLE IN APPENDIX C.	· ENSURE COMPLIANCE WITH RELEVANT AREAS CONCERNING ONLINE SAFETY AND CONTINUALLY LEARN FROM BEST PRACTICE AND THE WIDE RANGE OF ONLINE ADVICE THAT IS AVAILABLE. · NOTE THE LIST OF WEBSITES AND RESOURCES IDENTIFIED ON PAGE 95 OF THE DOCUMENT TO SUPPORT THIS. · ENGAGE WITH THE NSPCC CASPAR UPDATE SERVICE TO KEEP UP TO DATE WITH LATEST DEVELOPMENTS IN POLICY AND PRACTICE.
PREVENTING AND TACKLING BULLYING (DFE, 2017)	· NOTES THE EVOLVING NATURE OF CYBERBULLYING (p 8) AND THE POWERS SCHOOL STAFF HAVE IN TERMS OF EXAMINING MOBILE DEVICES. · ADDITIONAL GUIDANCE IS PROVIDED IN TERMS OF: - SCHOOLS PREVENTING AND RESPONDING TO CYBERBULLYING TARGETED AT SCHOOL STAFF;	· EXPLORE AND USE THE RESOURCES IDENTIFIED ON p 17 TO SUPPORT YOUR PROVISION.

POLICY	KEY POINTS	IMPLICATIONS FOR SCHOOLS
	- PARENTS AND CARERS PREVENTING AND RESPONDING TO CYBERBULLYING OF CHILDREN.	
SEXTING IN SCHOOLS AND COLLEGES (UKCCIS)	· AIMED AT SENIOR LEADERS AND EXPLAINS HOW TO RESPOND APPROPRIATELY TO INCIDENTS.	· ENGAGE WITH RELEVANT SECTIONS OF THE DOCUMENT. THIS ADDRESSES WORKING WITH A RANGE OF STAKEHOLDERS, AND YOU SHOULD CONSIDER THE PRACTICAL IMPLICATIONS FOR EACH CASE. · ENGAGE WITH FURTHER RESOURCES PUBLISHED BY THE UKCCIS, WHICH WILL ENSURE THAT THE SCHOOL'S STATUTORY DUTIES ARE FULFILLED.
OFSTED HANDBOOK (2018)	· THERE IS A FOCUS ON CHILDREN'S UNDERSTANDING OF HOW TO STAY SAFE ONLINE AND THE POTENTIAL DANGERS OF ONLINE ACTIVITY.	· ENSURE THESE ISSUES ARE FULLY EMBEDDED THROUGHOUT THE CURRICULUM TO ENSURE A COMPREHENSIVE UNDERSTANDING.
INTERNET SAFETY STRATEGY GREEN PAPER	· HIGHLIGHTS THE DIRECTION OF TRAVEL RELATED TO ONLINE SAFETY, INCLUDING WITHIN EDUCATION.	· REFLECT UPON YOUR CURRENT PRACTICE AND CONSIDER HOW IT MAY BE ENHANCED TO ENSURE BEST OUTCOMES.

1. Do you know about and understand the range of online resources that children use?

2. Do you understand the functionality of these applications, including the advantages they bring and the associated risks?

3. How will you use resources, such as NSPCC Net Aware, to develop your understanding and support the work you do with parents?

4. Are you aware of current online trends and how well equipped are you to embed these into your teaching as part of a broad and balanced curriculum?

5. Do you engage with data about online usage and trends to inform your provision and ensure relevance?

6. Through your teaching, do you consider a balance in terms of the benefits of online resources and their potential dangers?

7. To what extent do you empower children to take ownership of their online safety? How might you enhance your practice in this area?

8. How well equipped are your pupils to take informed responsibility for the information they share?

9. Do you make use of real-life analogies for the online world? How might you develop your practice here?

10. Do you provide opportunities for the children to reflect on the impact of the online world on all aspects of their well-being?

11. What do you do throughout your teaching to develop children's resilience, particularly to cope with issues stemming from online activity?

12. How do you engage with parents about online safety? What could you do to enhance your and the school's practice here?

13. How effectively do you model responsible online behaviour? How do you disseminate this to parents?

14. How can you ensure access to relevant support materials for all parents or carers?

15. Which online resources could you use to enhance parental engagement with the issues?

16. How effectively do you encourage and enable children to engage in meaningful talk about online safety issues? How might you enhance children's comfort and confidence in doing this?

17. Do you, the children and the parents know about reporting functions and how to use them when necessary?

18. How well do your pupils understand the laws around online activity and how might this be enhanced?

19. How well do you adhere to school policy associated with GDPR and, therefore, model best practice in this area?

20. How well do you encourage children to be respectful and responsible users of technology?

21. Which aspects of the Byron Review, relevant to your practice, need development and how might you work towards this?

22. How effectively is online activity monitored in your school to identify potential cyberbullying at an early stage?

23. What have you done to reduce instances of cyberbullying? What impact has this had? How might practice be enhanced?

24. Do you understand the language that children may use online and the potential implications of this?

25. How effectively does your school fulfil its statutory duties related to online safety?

26. How effective, relevant and up to date are your AUPs? How might these be enhanced?

Summary

Online safety is an ever-evolving issue and one which you need to keep up to date with. Online trends change frequently and you need to engage with resources to keep your knowledge current. It is very easy to focus on the negative elements, but you need to ensure a balanced perspective is developed with children and parents so they are empowered to understand the benefits as well as the dangers and how to mitigate against them. Open dialogue with all parties is needed to find out what children are doing online and to understand the functionality of apps with the aim of avoiding children being groomed and lured into danger. Ultimately, you need to model the behaviours that should be expected online to both children and their parents.

further reading and resources

UK Council for Child Internet Safety (UKCCIS) (www.gov.uk/government/ groups/uk-council-for-child-internet-safety-ukccis)	A wide range of resources to support best practice in online safety, including monitoring and questions for governors.
Childnet International (www.childnet. com) **KidSMART (www.kidsmart.org.uk)**	Comprehensive range of resources to support effective provision for online safety. Note the online safety calendar which shows how online safety can be a central feature of the curriculum throughout the year. KidSMART is part of this and teaches about online safety.
BBC Own It (www.bbc.com/ownit) **CBBC Curations: Stay Safe (www. bbc.co.uk/cbbc/findoutmore/ stay-safe-facts)**	Child-focused resources to support children in managing their safety online and developing confidence to tackle issues.
Be Internet Legends (https:// beinternetlegends.withgoogle.com/ en_uk)	A website that empowers children to make safe and informed choices regarding internet use.
Ealing Grid for Learning Online Safety toolkit for parents (www.egfl.org. uk/services-children/safeguarding-and-child-protection/safeguarding-specific-issues/online-safety-0)	Comprehensive guide to support parents/ carers in their work with children on online safety.
Safety Net Kids (www.safetynetkids. org.uk)	A child-focused website on all aspects of safety, including online issues.
NSPCC Online Safety (www.nspcc. org.uk/preventing-abuse/keeping-children-safe/online-safety) **Net Aware (www.net-aware.org.uk)**	Raises awareness of potential issues for teachers and parents/carers. Share Aware explores how to keep children safe online. Net Aware enables adults to remain up to date regarding children's social media use.
Think u Know (www.thinkuknow.co.uk)	The CEOP Centre's educational programme which is broken down for a range of users to provide appropriate resources per audience.
UK Safer Internet Centre (www. saferinternet.org.uk)	Hosts a range of resources to help children keep safe online.

Professionals Online Safety Helpline (www.saferinternet.org.uk/ professionals-online-safety-helpline)	A source of advice if concerns occur.
Bullying UK (www.bullying.co.uk)	A range of issues connected to bullying, including cyberbullying.
NSPCC (2017) Ten Years Since the Byron Review (https://learning.nspcc. org.uk/research-resources/2018/ 10-years-since-the-byron-review)	Review of progress since the Byron Review of 2008. Useful to identify where practice may need development.
South West Grid for Learning (https://swgfl.org.uk/products- services/online-safety/resources/ online-safety-policy-templates)	This site contains a wealth of guidance documents which can be accessed using the menu on the left hand side.

References

BBC (2018) 'Sharenting' Puts Young at Risk of Online Fraud. [online] Available at: www.bbc. co.uk/news/education-44153754 (accessed 10 April 2019).

Byron, T (2008) Safer Children in a Digital World: The Report of the Byron Review 2008. [online] Available at: https://webarchive.nationalarchives.gov.uk/20101008164914/www.dcsf.gov.uk/ byronreview/actionplan/index.shtml (accessed 10 April 2019).

Childnet (2018) 3-7-Year-Olds. [online] Available at: www.childnet.com/parents-and-carers/hot-topics/digital-wellbeing/3-7-year-olds (accessed 10 April 2019).

Children's Commissioner for England (2017) *Growing Up Digital*. London: Children's Commissioner for England.

Department for Education (2013) National Curriculum in England: Computing Programmes of Study. [online] Available at: www.gov.uk/government/publications/national-curriculum-in-england-computing-programmes-of-study (accessed 10 April 2019).

Department for Education (2017) *Preventing and Tackling Bullying*. London: DfE.

Department for Education (2018) *Keeping Children Safe in Education*. London: DfE.

Department of Health and Social Care (2018) Matt Hancock Warns of Dangers of Social Media on Children's Mental Health. [online] Available at: www.gov.uk/government/news/matt-hancock-warns-of-dangers-of-social-media-on-childrens-mental-health (accessed 10 April 2019).

The Guardian (2017) Revealed: The More Time That Children Chat on Social Media, the Less Happy They Feel. [online] Available at: www.theguardian.com/society/2017/apr/09/social-networks--children-chat-feel-less-happy-facebook-instagram-whatsapp (accessed 10 April 2019).

HM Government (2017) Internet Safety Strategy Green Paper. [online] Available at: www.gov.uk/government/consultations/internet-safety-strategy-green-paper (accessed 10 April 2019).

Lasher, S and Baker, C (2015) *Bullying: Evidence from the Longitudinal Study of Young People in England 2, Wave 2*. London: DfE.

NSPCC (2017a) *Net Aware Report 2017: Freedom to Express Myself Safely*. London: NSPCC.

NSPCC (2017b) *Ten Years Since the Byron Review: Are Children Safer in a Digital World?* London: NSPCC.

Ofcom (2017) *Children and Parents: Media Use and Attitudes Report*. London: Ofcom.

Phippen, A (2018) Abusive Comments One of the Main Causes of Upset for Young People Online. [online] Available at: https://swgfl.org.uk/magazine/abusive-comments-one-of-main-causes-of-upset-for-y/ (accessed 10 April 2019).

Smoothwall (2018) Insights. [online] Available at: www.smoothwall.com/company/resources/insights (accessed 20 November 2018).

UK Safer Internet Centre (2018) Digital Wellbeing – Guidance for Parents. [online] Available at: www.saferinternet.org.uk/blog/digital-wellbeing-%E2%80%93-guidance-parents (accessed 15 April 2019).

4. ADDRESSING ISSUES AROUND RADICALISATION

Key issues

Issues around radicalisation, extremism and terrorism are all around us and frequently make the news. While terrorism is nothing particularly new, it is an issue that increasingly impacts on all aspects of education and has significant implications for your daily practice. You have a legal and moral duty to ensure that issues around fundamental British values are embedded in your teaching across the curriculum in a bid to challenge views which may be considered extreme, providing balance and promoting mutual respect and tolerance. It is encouraging that there appears to be an increase in teachers' confidence when implementing the Prevent Duty (2015) according to research by Busher et al (2017) who found that most teachers in their survey felt very or fairly confident in implementing the Duty, largely due to being able to fit the requirements into existing practice.

This has become an increasing focus for schools given the current severe threat level to the UK from terrorism, meaning that a terrorist attack is highly likely. This has been the case for a number of years. The threat comes from a range of sources including far-right, neo-Nazi and white-supremacist groups, Daesh and Al-Qaeda ideologies, Irish nationalist and loyalist paramilitary groups, and groups linked to the animal-rights movement. These attacks may stem from large organisations or, increasingly, from lone attacks. This is not an issue associated with one group alone, and it is important to note that there are both international and domestic threats.

Definitions

As part of your duty for tackling radicalisation, it is important that you understand the following terms.

EXTREMISM

The Counter-Extremism Strategy (2015, p 9) defines extremism as, '*The vocal or active opposition to our fundamental values, including democracy, the rule of law, individual liberty and respect and tolerance for different faiths and beliefs.*' Calls for the death of members of the armed forces are also deemed extremist.

RADICALISATION

Educate Against Hate (2018) talks about radicalisation as a process through which a person comes to support terrorist activity or extreme ideologies that are associated with terrorist groups. This may be a result of pressure from someone and can manifest itself in attitude and conduct changes.

TERRORISM

The Terrorism Act of 2000 (HM Government, 2000) defines terrorism as action designed to influence the government or intimidate the public, done for the purpose of advancing a political, religious or ideological cause, which endangers or causes serious violence to people or property, or which seriously disrupts an electronic system.

While these elements are often presented in what appears to be a chronological order, it must be emphasised that one will not necessarily lead to the next, but there is potential for this to happen. Indeed, the whole notion of the Prevent Duty is to prevent this escalation through alertness to signals in order to prompt appropriate and timely intervention.

Government strategy

All of this work is driven by the government's Counter Terrorism Strategy, known as CONTEST (HM Government, 2018). This has recently been revised and notes the changing landscape since 2011, so it is essential that you remain up to date with developments that may impact on your practice. The aim of this is to, '*reduce the risk to the UK and its citizens and interests overseas from terrorism so that people can go about their lives freely and with confidence.*' There are four strands to this, which are:

1. prevent;
2. pursue;
3. protect; and
4. prepare.

All of these elements contribute to the larger picture related to terrorist activity, but the part that requires engagement from the education sector is Prevent. This centres around safeguarding children from being drawn into terrorism based on three key elements.

1. Ideology: those supporting terrorism need to be challenged.
2. Individual: preventing people from being lured into terrorism, ensuring access to advice and support.
3. Institution: supporting sectors and institutions where risks around radicalisation are evident.

CRITICISMS

There have been numerous critics of the Prevent Duty, often basing their denunciation on the over-targeting of particular groups which has led to distrust of the Duty by some communities. This has been magnified by how the media portrays terrorist incidents, which focuses on the religion of terrorists and in particular those from Muslim backgrounds. This has an inevitable impact on the general public's perception of what terrorism 'is' and has the potential to lead to some groups feeling marginalised, which can then lead to extremist views being developed. There remains much work to do to ensure that the Duty is delivered in a fair and proportionate manner so that no community feels targeted or alienated. The initiative is part of the wider safeguarding agenda, and it is essential that this remains at the forefront of your consciousness when implementing the Duty. Referring back to the idea of fundamental British values, it is essential that the notion of challenging stereotypes is embedded into your teaching as part of your work in promoting community cohesion. If we are to build communities that are future-proof, robust and resilient, you need to embed the feelings of belonging and cohesion into your classroom and wider school community.

In addition to these concerns, there is also a worry that the Prevent Duty stifles debate. In order to develop resilience, children need to engage in balanced discussions around critical issues. The Duty is intended to facilitate opportunities to discuss sensitive issues in a safe, informed and balanced environment. Sometimes these conversations may be difficult or sensitive, but if you do not provide the opportunity for these, the alternative of children finding their own way or talking to others who may lack balance but be very convincing could have potentially devastating consequences. It is perfectly acceptable for you to host visiting speakers, but it is essential that all visiting speakers are risk-assessed prior to booking to ensure that they will provide balanced input and thought. A good starting point for this is searching for them online and finding testimonies of their work. If there is any indication that they are one-sided and lack a balanced perspective, you should not use their services.

Vulnerabilities

A number of factors may increase a child's vulnerability to being drawn into radical or extreme thinking. Educate Against Hate (2018) notes that the assertions made by extremists may appeal to certain children's characteristics as they make these children feel valued. The factors that may make children susceptible to radicalisation include:

- identity issues;
- family influences;
- experiences of trauma or prejudice-based bullying;
- social issues;
- low self-esteem;
- influence of friends;
- online exposure to material that lacks balance.

It is important that you remain alert to these vulnerabilities and take note of any indications that a child may be being radicalised, particularly if they have a new group of friends, talk with passion about a particular issue or demonstrate a change in their usual behaviour.

The local context and risk assessment

The DfE advice document relating to Prevent (2015) makes it clear that schools must understand their local context in order to be able to mitigate against the risks. Risk will vary and is often subject to rapid change, but you must have regard for the fact that nowhere is completely risk-free. With news reports of terrorist activity, it is easy to assume where events are more likely to happen, which can lead to misconceptions and therefore complacency. To support this, all schools must have a Prevent risk assessment. The process of creating this document is as important as the resulting product. Good practice dictates that such policies should be developed by all staff, in consultation with key local partners, such as local police teams, community and religious groups. In the days of Google, it can be tempting to 'magpie' ideas from other schools. In the case of a Prevent risk assessment, this is not desirable or possible given that the local context and threat needs to be central. As previously noted, Prevent is not about stifling debate, but having the appropriate risk assessments in place is an essential aspect of fulfilling your legal obligations. Useful headings to form this risk assessment are:

- leadership;
- staff training;
- speakers and events;
- online safety;
- prayer/faith facilities;
- site security;
- safeguarding;
- communication;
- staff and volunteers;
- partnership working.

STAFF TRAINING

In addition to the risk assessment process and document, staff training is fundamental to ensuring schools meet the requirements set out by the DfE in *Keeping Children Safe in Education* to, '*be particularly alert to the potential need for early help for a child who . . . is at risk of being radicalised or exploited*' (2018, p 8). Training and engagement with the risk-assessment process will ensure that you understand the issues and how to approach them to ensure implementation of the Duty. The links to safeguarding are manifest, but your training should give you the knowledge to identify children who are at risk of being radicalised/drawn into terrorist activity, the skills to challenge extremist ideology and an awareness of how to refer children for support where necessary.

Notice, check, share, refer

These headings are the four stages of a referral process related to the Prevent Duty.

- Notice. First, you should note a concern about a child related to radicalisation or extremism.
- Check. You should then check for reasons for any changes in behaviour.
- Share. Sharing will be done through a conversation in which you discuss your concerns with a relevant colleague, notably the designated safeguarding lead.
- Refer. Following all of these stages, if the concern remains, the local authority Prevent team should be contacted to discuss your concerns in order to seek advice and support.

Engaging children with the news

As previously noted, when talking about challenging stereotypes, it is essential that you engage in meaningful and informed discussions about what is going on in the world so that children can begin to make sense of events and be reassured. A good starting point is the local context in terms of what the school does to keep everyone safe, including bomb drills, lock-down procedures and risk assessments. There can be a tendency to keep these from the children to avoid scaring them, but it is important that children understand the rationale for these activities as they show ways to keep themselves safe, thus bolstering resilience to cope with worries about events which are generally beyond their immediate control. Talk is important, and organisations including Childline, NSPCC and the Mental Health Foundation have produced resources to support you. Rosan (2018) for the Mental Health Foundation notes the following headline points to structure discussions both in school and at home about scary events.

- A news blackout is rarely helpful.
- Let them know the facts.
- Discourage overexposure.
- Let the children know they are safe.
- Let them know that it is normal to be concerned.
- Tailor the conversation to their age.
- Find the right time to talk about it.
- Leave lots of space for questions.
- Allow for repetition.
- Be as truthful as possible.

These points are further emphasised by *The Times* and NSPCC (2017) in their resource about talking to children about terrorism, noting that adults need to listen, allow children to ask questions, be honest, reassure and comfort. Hopefully these points will give you the confidence to do what is most important to help children understand: talk.

Good practice example

USING BREAKING/CURRENT NEWS STORIES TO CHALLENGE STEREOTYPES

When terrorist events make the news, use sources such as *BBC Newsround* or the children's newspaper *First News* to explore what has happened. You should talk about what has happened and why this might be, taking account of points made by the media coverage. First and foremost, it is essential to reassure children about what is being done to keep them safe through initiatives such as Prevent and how they can keep themselves safe. This is a good opportunity to link to learning in religious education about key religions and the messages these promote. If a particular group seems to be highlighted, refer to the key points of the text for that faith and then look at role models within that faith to combat negative stereotyping. This could be part of an ongoing display to recognise and celebrate diversity, reinforcing the need to challenge stereotypes in an attempt to respect and celebrate diversity.

The importance of education

In the national curriculum, the DfE (2013) notes key elements which are essential in preventing extremism and promoting integration:

- spiritual, moral, social and cultural education;
- equality (Equality Act 2010);
- fundamental British values (democracy, rule of law, individual liberty, mutual respect and tolerance of those of different faiths and beliefs);
- safeguarding.

All of these elements remain key Ofsted foci. None of these aspects exist in isolation and should be interwoven throughout all aspects of the curriculum. As such, throughout the curriculum you should be providing regular and meaningful opportunities for children to:

- reflect upon their personal beliefs and consider the impact of these;
- explore and improve their understanding of cultural diversity; showing respect and celebration for this;
- develop attitudes that complement British values so that they can contribute in a positive manner to life in modern Britain.

Good practice example

EMBEDDING KEY SKILLS TO DEVELOP CHILDREN'S RESILIENCE AND CRITICALITY IN HISTORY

The national curriculum for history states that,

Teaching should equip pupils to ask perceptive questions, think critically, weigh evidence, sift arguments, and develop perspective and judgement. History helps pupils to understand the complexity of people's lives, the process of change, the diversity of societies and relationships between different groups, as well as their own identity and the challenges of their time.

(DfE, 2013, p 188)

As a starting point, children should be allowed to identify an enquiry question as a basis for their historical investigation. We must remember that history is about interpretations, but often there is a focus on giving children 'the facts'. See yourself as the facilitator of learning rather than the controller of it. As children start to investigate their question, you should allow them to find (or provide them with) a range of sources and provide them with prompts to critically evaluate the material. You could ask questions such as the following examples.

- Who was it produced by?

- Why was it produced?

- What was the writer, illustrator, photographer trying to get the audience to think or believe?

- Is it complete?

- Is there an alternative view?

- What is fact and what is opinion?

- Based on known facts, which viewpoint is more likely?

These are just some examples as a starting point, but it is essential that, at all times, children are actively encouraged to justify their responses. Engaging children in digging beneath what is presented on the surface of historical evidence, they will understand the complexities involved in understanding what actually happened in the past. Through such activity, it is important that empathy is developed so that children can start to understand how it may have felt to be a particular person experiencing a particular event at a moment in time. This will support the development of respect for diversity. Regular and active engagement in these processes will not only support the development of historical knowledge, skill and understanding, but will also support you in fulfilling your duties concerned with the Prevent Duty in a really meaningful and engaging manner.

The notions of bias and untruth permeate all aspects of life, and it is crucial that your teaching engages children with appreciating these elements and being able to spot where this may be the case. Digital literacy is notable here with the rise in fake news. Children need to be able to engage critically with the information which they come across in order to develop a rounded and balanced understanding that does not take everything at face value.

THE WIDER CURRICULUM

In addition to the subjects children learn, wider curriculum issues need to be considered. The school environment should promote all of the values to promote cohesion, respect, tolerance and a sense of belonging in a vibrant and dynamic way. Assemblies should be used to address key issues, using appropriate speakers where applicable. There should be celebrations of all aspects of diversity which could be related to national events such as LGBT (Lesbian, Gay, Bisexual and Transgender) History Month, Black History Month and the like. At the heart of all of these activities should be the children. In terms of democracy, you should consider how children are actively engaged in the leadership and management of the school as well as how they take ownership of organising events to raise money for local, national and international charities.

Summary

Issues around the Prevent Duty are not going away. It is essential that you are fully trained and conversant with the local threat and issues relevant to your setting. As with all safeguarding, knowing your children and being alert to changes in their behaviours as possible signals of issues is paramount. There are numerous ways that the skills required for children to succeed in modern Britain can be integrated into the work you do with them across the curriculum.

Policy summary

POLICY	KEY POINTS	IMPLICATIONS FOR SCHOOLS
KEEPING CHILDREN SAFE IN EDUCATION (DFE, 2018)	· REFERS TO THE NEED FOR EARLY HELP, INCLUDING FOR CHILDREN WHO ARE AT RISK OF BEING RADICALISED OR EXPLOITED. · AS WITH ANYTHING RELATED TO SAFEGUARDING THE MESSAGE OF 'IT COULD HAPPEN HERE' IS REINFORCED.	· ENSURE COMPLIANCE WITH ALL ASPECTS RELATED TO ISSUES AROUND RADICALISATION. · CONTINUE TO KEEP UP TO DATE WITH EMERGING ISSUES AND NOTE CHANGES TO THE CONTEXT THAT MAY REQUIRE ATTENTION.
	· LOCAL AUTHORITIES MUST MAKE ENQUIRIES TO DECIDE WHETHER ANY ACTION IS NEEDED IF CHILDREN ARE SUFFERING OR LIKELY TO SUFFER SIGNIFICANT HARM, INCLUDING EXTRA-FAMILIAL THREATS LIKE RADICALISATION.	· REPORT ANY CONCERNS TO THE RELEVANT COLLEAGUES. · MAINTAIN VIGILANCE, INCLUDING LISTENING TO WHAT CHILDREN SAY AND DO. · KNOW YOUR CHILDREN AND ANY ISSUES CONCERNED WITH CONTEXTUAL SAFEGUARDING, WHICH MAY INCLUDE EXTREMIST CONCERNS ABOUT FAMILIES.

SHIFTING SANDS

POLICY	KEY POINTS	IMPLICATIONS FOR SCHOOLS
	· PAGE 15 NOTES CONTEXTUAL SAFEGUARDING, WHICH REFERS TO WIDER ENVIRONMENTAL FACTORS IN A CHILD'S LIFE THAT ARE A THREAT TO THEIR SAFETY OR WELFARE.	
THE PREVENT DUTY: DEPARTMENTAL ADVICE FOR SCHOOLS AND CHILDCARE PROVIDERS (DFE, JUNE 2015)	· EXPLAINS IMPLICATIONS OF THE PREVENT DUTY FOR PROFESSIONALS. · IDENTIFIES SOURCES OF INFORMATION, ADVICE AND SUPPORT.	· BE ALERT TO CHILDREN WHO MAY BE VULNERABLE TO RADICALISATION. · PROMOTE FUNDAMENTAL BRITISH VALUES AND DEVELOP CONFIDENCE/ RESILIENCE TO CHALLENGE EXTREMIST VIEWS. · PROVIDE A SAFE SPACE FOR CHILDREN TO ENGAGE IN DISCUSSIONS ABOUT DIFFICULT TOPICS. · ENGAGE WITH THE RISK ASSESSMENT PROCESS. · UNDERSTAND SCHOOL PROCEDURES AND ENGAGE WITH RELEVANT TRAINING.
OFSTED HANDBOOK (2018)	· THIS IS PART OF SAFEGUARDING IN TERMS OF PROMOTING WELFARE AND PREVENTING RADICALISATION AND EXTREMISM. IT COULD BE ARGUED THAT MOST ELEMENTS OF THE CRITERIA LINK TO THIS ISSUE, BUT THOSE OF PARTICULAR NOTE ARE: – OVERALL EFFECTIVENESS: TO BE OUTSTANDING A SCHOOL MUST SHOW *A THOUGHTFUL AND WIDE-RANGING PROMOTION OF PUPILS' SPIRITUAL, MORAL, SOCIAL AND CULTURAL DEVELOPMENT.'*	· CAREFULLY CONSIDER HOW YOUR CURRICULUM EMBEDS MEANINGFUL SMSC (SPIRITUAL, MORAL, SOCIAL AND CULTURAL) OPPORTUNITIES. · ENSURE REGULAR ENGAGEMENT WITH APPROPRIATE TRAINING. · ENSURE SWIFT RESPONSE TO ISSUES AND ADHERE TO REPORTING AND RECORDING PROTOCOLS.

POLICY	KEY POINTS	IMPLICATIONS FOR SCHOOLS
	- FOR OUTSTANDING LEADERSHIP AND MANAGEMENT, A SCHOOL MUST DEMONSTRATE: LEADERS' WORK TO PROTECT PUPILS FROM RADICALISATION AND EXTREMISM IS EXEMPLARY; LEADERS RESPOND SWIFTLY WHERE PUPILS ARE VULNERABLE TO THESE ISSUES; HIGH-QUALITY TRAINING DEVELOPS STAFF'S VIGILANCE, CONFIDENCE AND COMPETENCY TO CHALLENGE PUPILS' VIEWS AND ENCOURAGE DEBATE.	· PROVIDE MEANINGFUL OPPORTUNITIES FOR BALANCED DISCUSSION AND DEBATE ABOUT CONTROVERSIAL ISSUES.

❖ Critical questions

1. How confident do you feel about implementing the Prevent Duty in your practice?

2. How effectively do you keep up to date with developments in this area?

3. How do you ensure that you implement the Duty in a fair and proportionate manner?

4. How effectively do you embed the challenging of stereotypes into your teaching? Is there any potential to enhance this aspect of your practice?

5. How can you embed meaningful, critically balanced discussion around key issues into your practice?

6. Are you alert to children who may be vulnerable to being radicalised?

7. Is there anything that you need to do about any concerns you may have?

8. To what extent were you involved in the creation of your school's risk assessment related to Prevent?

9. How confident are you in your understanding of the local context?

10. Which training related to tackling radicalisation have you engaged with and how have you adapted your practice as a result?

11. How effective have you found the notice, check, share and refer process? Is there any way this could be enhanced in your setting?

12. What could you do with parents and carers to develop a shared and consistent approach to talking about distressing news with children?

13. How effectively are SMSC and FBV (fundamental British values) integrated into your teaching? How might this be enhanced?

14. To what extent do you control and to what extent do you facilitate children's learning? How can you enhance your facilitator role to develop children's confidence to fully engage with complex issues and questions?

15. How often do you give children the opportunity to develop their confidence and resilience by asking them to justify their opinions?

16. How effectively do your pupils question the reliability and validity of information with which they are presented?

17. Which aspects of FBV are particular strengths in your school and which require development? How might these developments be realised?

further reading and resources

Educate Against Hate (https://educateagainsthate.com)	A website that is continually developing to provide practical advice about protecting children from extremism and radicalisation with dedicated areas for teachers, parents and school leaders.
***The Times* and the NSPCC, How Should You Talk to Your Children About Terrorism? (www.thetimes.co.uk/nspcc/index.html)**	Guidance about how you can talk to children about terrorist events in the news. Aimed at parents, but the issues are transferrable to anyone working with children.
Online Home Office Prevent training package (www.elearning.prevent.homeoffice.gov.uk)	An online training package to develop your understanding of issues around tackling radicalisation. This enables you to download a certificate upon completion and helps to show engagement with the issues.
Prevent for Schools (www.preventforschools.org)	Lancashire Safeguarding Board site which offers a range of phase-specific practical resources and guidance to support schools' work around the Prevent Duty.

South West Grid for Learning (https://swgfl.org.uk/magazine/extreme-measures)	SWGFL produces a range of helpful, practically focused materials with ideas about how to protect children from online extremism.
Childline Worries about the World (https://childline.org.uk/info-advice/your-feelings/anxiety-stress-panic/worries-about-the-world)	This website addresses all elements of the Prevent Duty as applicable to children and provides helpful practical guidance about addressing issues sensitively but openly with children.
Mental Health Foundation, Talking to Your Children About Scary World News (www.mentalhealth.org.uk/publications/talking-to-your-children-scary-world-news)	Practical advice about how to engage children in open discussions about scary world news in order to minimise the negative impact it has upon children.

References

Busher, J, Choudhury, T, Thomas, P and Harris, G (2017) What the Prevent Duty Means for Schools and Colleges in England: An Analysis of Educationalists' Experiences. [online] Available at: http://azizfoundation.org.uk/wp-content/uploads/2017/07/What-the-Prevent-Duty-means-for-schools-and-colleges-in-England.pdf (accessed 10 April 2019).

Department for Education (2013) The National Curriculum. [online] Available at: https://assets.publishing.service.gov.uk/government/uploads/system/uploads/attachment_data/file/425601/PRIMARY_national_curriculum.pdf (accessed 10 April 2019).

Department for Education (2015) The Prevent Duty: Departmental Advice for Schools and Childcare Providers. London: DfE.

Department for Education (2018) Keeping Children Safe in Education. London: DfE.

Educate Against Hate (2018) Who Is Vulnerable? [online] Available at: https://educateagainsthate.com/teachers/which-children-and-young-people-are-vulnerable-to-radicalisation/ (accessed 10 April 2019).

HM Government (2000) The Terrorism Act 2000 (United Kingdom of Great Britain and Northern Ireland). [online] Available at: www.legislation.gov.uk/ukpga/2000/11/contents (accessed 10 April 2019).

HM Government (2015) Counter-extremism Strategy. London: HM Government.

HM Government (2015) Revised Prevent Duty Guidance for England and Wales. London: HM Government.

HM Government (2018) CONTEST: The United Kingdom's Strategy for Countering Terrorism. [online] Available at: https://assets.publishing.service.gov.uk/government/uploads/system/uploads/attachment_data/file/716907/140618_CCS207_CCS0218929798-1_CONTEST_3.0_WEB.pdf (accessed 10 April 2019).

NSPCC (2017) Supporting Children Worried About Terrorism. [online] Available at: www.nspcc.org.uk/what-we-do/news-opinion/supporting-children-worried-about-terrorism/ (accessed 10 April 2019).

Rosan, C (2018) Talking to Your Children About Scary World News. [online] Available at: www.mentalhealth.org.uk/publications/talking-to-your-children-scary-world-news (accessed 10 April 2019).

5. WHY IS RELATIONSHIPS AND SEX EDUCATION SO IMPORTANT?

Key issues

This chapter considers recent and forthcoming developments concerning relationships and sex education (RSE), with a particular emphasis on the relationships aspect at primary level. It builds upon cases of children's sexual misconduct and tackles issues around peer-on-peer abuse. You will develop a practical understanding of strategies that you may use to enhance children's confidence and resilience to deal with issues in a safe, confident and assertive manner. There has been a move towards placing a greater emphasis on relationships in an attempt to reinforce the need for teaching to be based on the notion of positive relationships.

We are constantly hearing about how the world is changing, not least with regards to technology. With advances in technology, particularly, there is a real need to review the way in which we equip children to understand issues around health and relationships in an accurate and balanced manner. From September 2020, there will be new guidance to structure teaching about positive and safe relationships. All schools will be required to teach about good mental and physical health as well as online and offline safety and the need for healthy relationships. From that date all children will study compulsory health education and reformed relationships education in primary. Damian Hinds (DfE, 2018b) has a clear vision to ensure children are well prepared for life in modern Britain, clearly stating that, *'Part of this is making sure that they are informed about how to keep themselves safe and healthy and have good relationships with others.'*

Why the change?

The previous guidance was published in 2000, and there is a clear need to update this to reflect current issues in society so as to help prepare children for life in modern Britain. The Children's Society (2017, p 1) makes the following points:

Statutory guidance on SRE (sex and relationships education) was last updated 17 years ago and is not representative of the contemporary issues children and young people experience online, nor does it address safer sex and healthy relationships for protected groups outlined in the Equalities Act 2010. Guidance must be updated in collaboration with young people to make sure that SRE equips them with the knowledge they need to keep themselves safe and enjoy happy and healthy relationships now, and in the future.

Links to safeguarding

Keeping Children Safe in Education (DfE, 2018a) highlights the range of issues that you need to be aware of and address, such as sexual harassment, sexual violence and peer-on-peer abuse, all of which may occur face to face or in an online context. Children's awareness and identification of what constitutes inappropriate behaviour, contact or treatment are key to being able to address in your teaching the issues as they arise. The new guidance should support schools in enhancing practice in this area. It states that for teaching to be effective, *'core knowledge is broken down into units of manageable size and communicated clearly to pupils in a carefully sequenced way, with a planned programme of lessons'* (DfE, 2019).

The content will need to be planned through schemes of work which are progressive and adapted to the needs of the children. There will be flexibility for you and your school to organise the curriculum in the best way to meet the needs of your school context. The key features of an effective curriculum around these issues are:

- relatability;
- relevance to lived experiences;
- participatory;
- that the content helps children to understand the world around them.

Opportunities for parents/carers

The issues that you will be exploring are sensitive and far-reaching. For some children and their families, they may resonate more, depending on their life experiences. You will need to teach about these issues in a confident and unembarrassed way. You will not have all the answers and may have limited experience of some of the issues, but this is fine. There is a real opportunity here to engage with parents and carers and involve the children in curriculum design and content so that safeguarding can be proactively promoted and enacted. Parental engagement also has the potential to enrich the whole school approaches related to bullying, equality issues, behaviour and pupil well-being. Javed Khan, Chief Executive of Barnardo's (cited by DfE, 2018b), emphasises the importance of regular communication with parents in order to enable them to feel reassured about what their children are being taught. In addition to this, there is a range of resources to support your teaching available from September 2019.

Types of relationships

There is a great diversity in types of relationships, and relationships education needs to take account of these, which include:

- healthy relationships;
- family relationships;
- same-sex relationships;
- friendships;
- strangers.

Intimate relationships are not included in the primary curriculum but will be part of RSE at secondary. It is important that children are supported in understanding what makes for a healthy relationship in the various types of relationship they might encounter. As part of the carefully structured curriculum, you will need to consider how relationships may evolve or change at various points, such as the transition between primary and secondary school. It is at points like these that having a secure grasp of what is a healthy relationship and where there may be potential danger is going to be instrumental in ensuring children continue to grow up and develop in a safe and supportive environment.

Good practice example

PRIMARY TO SECONDARY TRANSITION

Use the NSPCC lesson plans which are aimed at Year 6 children to support the transition from primary to secondary education (https://learning.nspcc.org.uk/research-resources/schools/making-sense-relationships).

1. Secondary school: empowering children to deal with the challenges of moving from primary to secondary school.
2. Changing friendships: looks at the concept of friendship, identifying the positive aspects of new friendships and how to manage friendships in a positive, safe and healthy manner.
3. Healthy online friendships: empowering children to recognise how to keep online friendships healthy.

The importance of including same-sex relationships in the curriculum was emphasised by Amanda Spielman (BBC, 2019) in that children should be taught to understand that some people marry someone of the same sex and that some children may have two mummies or two daddies. In terms of preparing children to live confident lives in the future, Spielman said, '*It's about making sure that children who do happen to realise that they themselves may not fit a conventional pattern know that they're not bad or ill.*' You need to be confident in your delivery of this aspect of the curriculum, as detailed in Chapter 7. It is important to remember that this is not about the sexual aspect of relationships; it is about understanding, respecting and celebrating the diversity of relationships in society, in line with the Equality Act of 2010.

Healthy relationships

It is essential that children understand the features of a healthy, safe and happy relationship as well as signs that a relationship may be, or has the potential to become, toxic. In addition to understanding the features of a healthy relationship, children need to be able to establish and develop these. The key features of healthy relationships include:

- self-respect;
- consideration and respect for others;
- turn-taking;
- kindness;
- honesty;
- truthfulness;
- commitment;
- tolerance;
- clear boundaries and an understanding of privacy for individuals;
- consent in terms of permission seeking and giving; and
- an ability to manage and resolve conflict.

These are significant areas and will require regular reinforcement from an early stage throughout the curriculum but need to have a specific focus through relationships education. The guidance (DfE, 2019) talks about age-appropriate ways of developing these concepts, for example, '*understanding one's own and others' boundaries in play, in negotiations about space, toys, resources and so on.'* In addition to your teaching, you should also be providing a model of the highest standards of personal conduct that proactively demonstrate the attributes of a healthy relationship. The guidance (DfE, 2019) clearly states what children should know by the end of primary school in relation to the following areas:

- families and people who care for me;
- caring friendships;
- respectful relationships;
- online relationships; and
- being safe.

The ultimate aim of all of this is to prevent, as a result of children having a greater awareness, incidents of domestic violence, controlling or coercive behaviour, FGM, forced marriage and honour-based violence. Of course, there is potential for children to disclose experiences during the course of their learning about healthy relationships. If this happens, as usual, you must follow your school's safeguarding policy about reporting disclosures.

Good practice example

TEACHING ABOUT HEALTHY RELATIONSHIPS

The NSPCC has produced a resource entitled, *It's Not OK* (https://learning.nspcc.org.uk/research-resources/schools/its-not-ok). This is aimed at Key Stage 3 children, but, depending on your context and the issues currently being faced by your children, some of the principles and content may be relevant. The authors of the resource note that it may be adapted for different audiences.

The resource is designed to enable children to spot the features of relationships and to note worrying behaviour. It covers issues including:

- online safety;
- grooming;
- sexting;
- harmful sexual behaviour;
- child sexual abuse; and
- CSE.

You might not use the resources, but you could use the ideas as a basis for your teaching.

A healthy relationship will enable the people involved to talk openly and share concerns. Families will usually be the most appropriate forum for discussing concerns, but if the issues are based on forms of abuse relevant to the culture of the family, this will not be ideal. Children need to understand that there are people, such as teachers, who they can speak to about any relationship concerns in safety. They also need to be aware of support available through organisations such as Childline and the NSPCC.

Technology and online relationships

Increasingly, children are engaging with a range of technology from an early age. It is important that you keep up to date with how children are establishing various relationships online through resources like the NSPCC Net Aware and Share Aware resources as discussed in Chapter 3. There are very strong links to online safety issues here. Not only will you need to teach about the management of relationships, but you will also need to explore the ways in which data may be used to develop a meaningful understanding of how to use technology safely and keep personal information private.

Sex education in primary schools

Sex education is not compulsory in primary schools, whereas relationships education will be. Primary schools have a choice about what to teach regarding sex education based on the needs of the children in any particular school. Aspects of sex education that need to be covered, include:

- puberty as part of health education;
- subject content in science, eg, external body parts, the growth of the human body; and reproduction in plants and animals.

Your school's approach to sex education needs to prepare children for the changes they will experience through puberty and understand how a baby is conceived and born. The guidance (DfE, 2019) promotes active consultation with parents to ensure that parents are equipped to talk to their children about sex education based on an understanding of what they will be taught in school. The clarity of the policy and communication with parents are essential, particularly if aspects of sex education are taught that transcend the primary science national curriculum.

PARENTAL RIGHT TO WITHDRAW CHILDREN

If a school chooses to teach sex education beyond the science national curriculum, parents have the right to withdraw their children from these lessons. There was a recent case at a Birmingham primary school that saw parental protests concerning teaching about same-sex relationships. The DfE (2019) is very clear that parents have the right to withdraw their child from sex education if included as part of relationships (and sex) education, but they cannot withdraw children from relationships education.

FAITH SCHOOLS

The age of children and their religious background are key factors when ensuring the appropriateness of RSE content. The tenets of the given faith will be allowed to be used as a basis for RSE in these settings, but they must still comply with the underpinning principles of the Equality Act of 2010, for example by showing respect and tolerance for those with protected characteristics, such as people who are LGBT.

Physical health and mental well-being

These elements are included because of the link between physical and mental health. As mentioned in Chapter 9, it is important that discussions around mental health are seen as normal. The key elements to be included are:

- the benefits of daily exercise;
- good nutrition and sufficient sleep;
- enabling children to have the language to understand the range of emotions and articulate how they are feeling;
- enabling children to judge whether what they are feeling and how they are behaving is appropriate and proportionate for the situations that they experience.

(DfE, 2019)

The guidance (DfE, 2019) clearly states what children should know about physical health and mental well-being by the end of primary school:

- mental well-being;
- internet safety and harms;
- physical health and fitness;
- healthy eating;
- drugs, alcohol and tobacco;
- health and prevention;
- basic first aid; and
- changing adolescent body.

Summary

This is a significant area that you will need to develop in preparation for September 2020. You are probably already doing some great work that will help to address the requirements, so it would be good to audit what you currently teach to identify areas of good practice as well as any gaps. Staff confidence is a key feature that needs to be considered to ensure effective teaching. There will be expertise within your school that should be shared and could be used as part of the training process. Now is also a good time to be engaging with children and their parents or carers to identify the areas that need to be included within your curriculum and any concerns that stakeholders have so that you can begin to consider how they may be overcome. Avoid assuming what is needed. Engage in genuine discussions to give you a solid foundation on which to build a meaningful and relevant curriculum. The issues associated with relationships (and sex) education are sensitive, and having a whole-school approach with buy-in from all stakeholders will enable you to develop a curriculum that meets the needs of your children and context.

Policy summary

POLICY	KEY POINTS	IMPLICATIONS FOR SCHOOLS
KEEPING CHILDREN SAFE IN EDUCATION (2018)	· STATUTORY GUIDANCE FOR ALL SCHOOLS.	· ENSURE THAT YOUR R(S)E CURRICULUM ENGAGES CHILDREN WITH THE ISSUES SO THAT THEY ARE ABLE TO IDENTIFY WHEN RELATIONSHIPS OR THE ACTIONS OF OTHERS MAY BE A CAUSE FOR CONCERN.
RELATIONSHIPS EDUCATION, RSE AND HEALTH EDUCATION GUIDANCE (DFE, 2019)	· THIS IS GUIDANCE ABOUT WHAT NEEDS TO BE TAUGHT, INCLUDING THE END OF PRIMARY EXPECTATIONS FOR EACH ELEMENT.	· AUDIT CURRENT PROVISION AND CONSIDER ELEMENTS OF GOOD PRACTICE WHICH CAN BE BUILT UPON AS WELL AS AREAS WHICH MAY REQUIRE DEVELOPMENT. · THIS MAY RELATE TO CURRICULUM PROVISION OR STAFF KNOWLEDGE, UNDERSTANDING OR CONFIDENCE. BEGIN TO IDENTIFY RESOURCES TO SUPPORT YOUR IMPLEMENTATION OF THIS REQUIREMENT FROM SEPTEMBER 2020.

POLICY	KEY POINTS	IMPLICATIONS FOR SCHOOLS
OFSTED (FROM SEPTEMBER 2019)	· THE RELEVANT AREAS OF THE FRAMEWORK APPEAR TO BE: - BEHAVIOUR AND ATTITUDES: CHILDREN ARE RESILIENT TO SETBACKS; RELATIONSHIPS AMONGST LEARNERS AND STAFF REFLECT A POSITIVE AND RESPECTFUL CULTURE; LEARNERS FEEL SAFE AND DO NOT EXPERIENCE DISCRIMINATION.	· ENSURE THAT YOUR CURRICULUM PROVISION EXPLICITLY DEVELOPS ALL OF THESE ATTRIBUTES.
	· PERSONAL DEVELOPMENT: REFERS TO CHARACTER DEVELOPMENT, INCLUDING RESILIENCE, CONFIDENCE AND INDEPENDENCE; CHILDREN KNOW HOW TO KEEP PHYSICALLY AND MENTALLY HEALTHY; CHILDREN ARE PREPARED FOR LIFE IN MODERN BRITAIN IN THAT THEY ARE ACTIVE, RESPECTFUL AND RESPONSIBLE CITIZENS.	

❖ Critical questions

1. What do you already do to engage children with the notion of healthy, happy, safe, productive and equal relationships?

2. Why do you consider relationships education to be particularly important in the context of your school setting?

3. What are your priorities and actions to support preparations for full implementation from September 2020?

4. What do you consider your training needs to be at this juncture?

5. How will you engage with children and parents or carers to ensure the relevance of the curriculum that you offer?

6. Do you already have resources that could support curriculum delivery for relationships education?

7. How confident do you feel about developing children's resilience? Do you feel the need for any training in this area and what form might this take?

8. Are there any aspects of dealing with same-sex relationships that you need to recap?

9. How are the features of positive relationships reinforced throughout the curriculum at all stages in your school?

10. How do you ensure children understand the full range of people who they may approach to discuss relationship concerns?

11. How well do you understand the range of ways in which children engage and develop relationships online?

further reading and resources

Childline (www.childline.org.uk)	A range of resources, including advice about family relationships.
NSPCC (www.nspcc.org.uk)	A range of resources that provide information about key issues related to this topic.
NSPCC PANTS (www.nspcc.org.uk/preventing-abuse/keeping-children-safe/underwear-rule)	A resource to engage children with the idea of sexual abuse and to understand their rights and how to keep themselves safe.
Growing up with Yasmine and Tom (www.fpa.org.uk/relationships-and-sex-education/growing-up-with-yasmine-and-tom)	A subscription-based resource to support the teaching of relationships education in primary schools.
Women's Aid, The Hideout (http://thehideout.org.uk)	A resource to help children understand domestic abuse and how to take action against it.

Barnardo's Real Love Rocks (www. barnardosrealloverocks.org.uk/ pro-primary-school-resource)	A resource to develop children's understanding about healthy, happy and safe relationships. The resource has four sections: (1) healthy and equal relationships; (2) grooming; (3) keeping safe; (4) online safety.

At the time of writing, there are limited resources available to support relationships education at primary level, but more are set to be available from September 2019.

References

BBC (2019) Ofsted Says Schools Should Teach Pupils About Same-Sex Couples. [online] Available at: www.bbc.co.uk/news/uk-england-birmingham-47282724 (accessed 5 April 2019).

Children's Society (2017) The Importance of Sex and Relationships Education. [online] Available at: www.childrenssociety.org.uk/sites/default/files/tcs-briefing-sex-and-relationships-education_.pdf (accessed 22 February 2019).

Department for Education (2018a) *Keeping Children Safe in Education*. London: DfE.

Department for Education (2018b) New Relationships and Health Education in Schools. [online] Available at: www.gov.uk/government/news/new-relationships-and-health-education-in-schools (accessed 22 February 2019).

Department for Education (2019) Relationships Education, Relationships and Sex Education (RSE) and Health Education: Guidance for Governing Bodies, Proprietors, Head Teachers, Principals, Senior Leadership Teams, Teachers. [online] Available at: https://consult.education.gov.uk/pshe/relationships-education-rse-health-education/supporting_documents/20170718_%20Draft%20guidance%20for%20consultation.pdf (accessed 22 February 2019).

Murray, N (2019) Majority Feel Teaching Resilience in the Classroom Is a Flawed Concept. [online] Available at: www.mentalhealthtoday.co.uk/news/teach-me-well/majority-feel-teaching-resilience-in-the-classroom-is-a-flawed-concept (accessed 22 February 2019).

6. GENDER AND IDENTITY

Key issues

The issue of gender, particularly trans identities, is increasingly coming to the fore. Sadly, a lack of representation through popular culture leads to ignorance, lack of understanding and even fear. This is hopefully set to change with a growing number of campaigns linked to the experiences of trans people and an enhanced visibility of a range of experiences. Education incorporating the full range of identities from an early age is essential if you are to bring about the acceptance that is required. While there is no easy, one-size-fits-all solution, this chapter will explore the issues that children may face in relation to gender and will consider strategies to support your practice in this area. With the recent publication of documents including the LGBT Action Plan (Government Equalities Office [GEO], 2018a), Gender Separation in Schools (DfE, 2018) and the consultation on the Gender Recognition Act of 2004, now really is the time to reconsider how you deal with the thorny issue of gender identity.

Defining gender

Gender is a social construct whereby society has been conditioned to associate certain characteristics with gender, often linked to biological sex. This leads to stereotypical assumptions about how people should behave from birth, based on perceived societal norms, but people do not always conform to these. People may feel confined by such stereotypes. There is a clear distinction between sex and gender. Sex relates to biology whereas gender is much more individual in terms of how one feels and wants to be known by others. Gender is not a binary concept, even though it is often seen as such: it is more of a spectrum (Educational Action Challenging Homophobia [EACH], 2016). The spectrum is varied and includes identities including trans, non-binary, gender fluid, gender questioning and many more. People may express their gender in a range of ways, including through their actions, clothes and preferred pronouns. It is absolutely essential that you respect the pronouns selected by individuals to show acceptance and that you see each individual how they wish to be seen.

Buzzfeed's video *The Gender Machine* (Branson, 2016) explains gender using the analogy of red and blue toys being made by a machine that, on occasion, makes purple toys. The notion is that the purple toys have to fit into existing, predefined groups. It reinforces the importance of talk to recognise and celebrate diversity so that eventually the predefined barriers are broken down and people are not compartmentalised. This provides a powerful message, ending with food for thought when the machine produces a green toy!

Good practice example

USING ONLINE VIDEOS TO CHALLENGE GENDER STEREOTYPING BEHAVIOURS

Children are now accessing online videos, including YouTube, so this is a good way of tapping into their interests. The Always company has been leading on a hashtag campaign, #LikeAGirl, which challenges the stereotype 'like a girl', which tends to imply weakness and inferiority. Prior to showing the video (www.youtube.com/watch?v=XjJQBjWYDTs), ask children questions that are posed in the video to find their initial ideas, eg, mime running, fighting and throwing like a girl. Lead a discussion about how it may feel to hear this expression and challenge the language that people often use without thinking.

This idea can be adapted depending upon your context and could be used to address words and phrases used by the children, perhaps in the playground. The important thing is to challenge language and unpick the meaning, considering the potential impact on self-esteem and confidence in order to use language more appropriately.

USING STORY TO REINFORCE THE IMPORTANCE OF CHALLENGING GENDER STEREOTYPES

Story is an excellent way of addressing key issues with children. They can also support coverage of key curriculum requirements too. In this example, the story of astronaut Sally Ride (in Brooks, 2018, p 168) can be used as part of a Key Stage 1 history topic about significant individuals while also addressing issues around gender and identity.

Share the story with the class. Perhaps use images and role play to bring the story to life. Just before the part that identifies some of the questions Ride was asked by journalists, engage the children in paired talk to consider questions they may have asked her if they had been journalists at the time. Compare their responses. Identify those that contain potential stereotypes and reflect on the appropriateness of this. Talk about how the story tells us about Ride laughing at the questions or ignoring them entirely. How might such questions have made her feel and what possible impacts could such questions have?

Talk about the legacy of Sally Ride and why it is important as well as why it has been so successful.

The children could follow this up by representing the message they have taken away from the story about gender and identity in any way they choose. This choice will reinforce the point about different people choosing to express themselves in different ways, each method being valid.

Acknowledging the issue

This issue is one that is very present in schools. There are children identifying as trans from early years, and this has to be respected. As a result of a lack of education and exposure to a range of gender identities generally, there tends to be high rates of bullying, with Stonewall (2017a) reporting 64 per cent of trans pupils in Britain's schools being bullied and only 40 per cent of LGBT pupils reporting that their schools say transphobic bullying is wrong. There is clearly much to do here in terms of getting the message across. Bullying can impact on school attendance, and the implications for trans children and young people to fulfil their potential are negative. It could also be argued that there has been a lack of training and guidance for schools which has resulted in them not handling the issue appropriately or, at worst, at all. Now really is the time to work on this.

The legal context

As with LGBT issues, a key concern that teachers have about dealing with sensitive issues, in this case gender identity, is the potential reaction of parents. The Equality Act of 2010 is key here as any education around and inclusion of the full range of gender identities and the challenging of transphobic behaviour fulfils your duties in ensuring that no one is discriminated against based on any protected characteristic.

GENDER RECOGNITION ACT 2004

The Gender Recognition Act (GRA) of 2004 has long been regarded as out of date, particularly in terms of some terminology and the slow bureaucratic processes contained within. To this end, in 2018, the government ran an open consultation on proposed changes and sought views from everyone, with no lower age limit. The GEO (2018b) noted,

Since the GRA came into force, only 4,910 people have legally changed their gender. This is fewer than the number of trans respondents to the government's LGBT survey, who were clear that they wanted legal recognition but had not applied because they found the current process too bureaucratic, expensive and intrusive.

This reflects the scale of the issue and the urgent need for reformed legislation to move things forward, to act as a springboard for greater recognition by society. The proposed changes ultimately seek new rights for transgender and non-binary people to create a more equal society and simplify the process for someone wishing to change their gender. The legal recognition of an individual's gender identity, it is hoped, will ease social inclusion and acceptance from others. Stonewall (2018) played a key role in promoting engagement with the consultation, stating that they supported a reformed act that:

- requires no medical diagnosis or evidence to be presented for young people to have their identity legally recognised;
- recognises non-binary identities; and
- gives all trans people, including 16–17 year-olds, the right to self-determine through simpler, streamlined administrative processes.

Language

The language associated with gender is nuanced, contextual, complex, ever-evolving and must be used with care and respect. It is essential that you consider what is appropriate in terms of language on a case-by-case basis. The It Gets Better Project (2018) has produced a glossary of key terms which are summarised here.

- Binary: male or female.
- Cisgender: where gender identity matches sex assigned at birth.
- Gender non-conforming: where gender identity and expression do not match societal expectations. This umbrella term includes the following:
  - agender: no connection with gender;
  - bigender: identifies with male and female identities;
  - gender fluid: identity varies over time;
  - genderqueer/third gender: expression or identity falls outside of male and female;
  - intergender: someone who is either a combination of genders or in between;
  - pangender: comprises a range of identities.
- Intersex: has a sexual anatomy that does not match typical male or female definitions. They may or may not identify with the gender they were assigned at birth.
- Questioning: will be questioning their gender.
- Transgender: gender identity or expression differs to the sex they were assigned at birth.
- Transition: this is a very personal choice and will not be the same for everyone. This relates to how someone changes their gender expression to match their identity. It may involve the use of a different name or pronouns, choice of dress, hormone therapy or surgery.

PRONOUNS

Pronouns are so important when talking about gender identities. They can be the difference between someone feeling valued, accepted and included or ostracised and not seen as a real person. One set identified by the It Gets Better Project (2018) is 'they', 'them' and 'their'. These are gender-neutral singular pronouns, used in place of 'he' or 'she', 'him' or 'her', and 'his' or 'hers'. There are numerous online videos, including that produced by EACH (2016), which show young people telling of how people's failure to recognise or respect their individual choice of pronouns or even their name has adversely affected their self-esteem and sense of worth as an individual person. Pronouns are an individual choice, so you should not assume. It is so easy to ask an individual what their chosen pronouns are that you can then use with respect. This will make the world of difference to that individual and needs to be emphasised with all stakeholders.

Media representation

It is widely acknowledged, including by Stonewall (2017a) that representation in the media is broadly lacking, with a narrow range of experiences being portrayed, often with a focus on glamorised celebrity or medical transitions. As a result of this, the experiences of most trans people are missing from our lives and experience, including non-medical transitions, non-binary people or gender variance, which results in ignorance and prejudice. In the autumn of 2018, ITV showed a drama entitled *Butterfly* which was based on a family with a trans child who was going through the transitioning process. This received mixed press, but its importance is emphasised by the following reviews. '*Many LGBT young people say watching LGBT shows and/or movies helps them to embrace their identity as an LGBT young person*' (Stein, 2018). Tate (2018) in *The Telegraph* stated, '*But it was an unarguably well-intended, carefully calibrated pushback against lazy prejudice or rushes to judgement, never soft-pedalling the difficulties for everyone involved. If it helps one child or parent, then it will have done its job.'*

Links to LGB issues

Stonewall (2017b) recognises that there are *'obvious overlaps of need, experience and potential learning'* but also notes the specific difficulties that transgender people may experience. Stonewall is clear that a trans identity does not equate to sexual orientation and, therefore, needs to have its own prominence, but notes that trans people may also be LGB. It is important that you treat these issues, while being related and holding common themes, as distinct. You should consider where it is possible to include trans people and experiences as part of your broad, balanced curriculum to ensure that a range of experiences are included as part of your teaching. This has the potential to break down the barriers and prejudices that exist as well as make trans or questioning children feel valued and accepted. The ultimate aim of all of this relates very much to Stonewall's (2017b) vision of *'a society where transphobia is unacceptable and is challenged by everyone.'*

In the classroom

You will often hear people saying that it is not appropriate for young children to learn about such things, but early education is a key factor in moving forward to the acceptance needed in society. Any education should relate back to the children and their own experiences. With gender, you can talk about the stereotypes that exist around boys and girls and use stories, such as *It's Okay to Be Different* by Todd Parr, to engage them in discussion about what makes them special and why they should be proud of themselves. Children need to be given opportunities to develop an understanding of who they are, recognising and celebrating the fact that everyone is different. The curriculum, displays, environment and ethos of the school are so important in terms of creating a safe, accepting and supporting place for the children to grow as confident and respectful, tolerant individuals. It is not enough to do a tokenistic isolated lesson that refers to a trans person. These elements need to be integrated and reinforced routinely throughout the whole curriculum for them to have an impact and reduce the stigma that may be attached to issues (Stonewall, 2017b).

AWARENESS

Be open to the fact that you may have a questioning or trans child in your class who may be open about their identity or may be concealing this through fear of ridicule. Those opportunities to recognise the range of identities can make a world of difference to these children. Something that you will do every day is group your children in some way. How often do you deploy boy/girl groupings? If you do, consider how this may impact on questioning or trans children; which group do they go in? What will the reaction of the rest of that group potentially be? There are numerous possibilities for alternative ways to group that will not impact on their sense of belonging or identity, such as birth month, alphabetical order by name – and the list goes on.

As with homophobia or biphobia, it is essential that you and all colleagues are trained to be alert to potential transphobic actions or language. Use of words such as 'tranny' or inappropriate questions, 'So, what have you got "down there"?' need to be challenged each and every time they are heard to promote the respect and tolerance that is needed to enable all young people, regardless of their identity, to flourish.

Broader issues, such as the school's uniform policy, may need to be reconsidered if it is gender specific as might toilet and changing facilities to ensure inclusion for all. Many of these might have been accepted practices for a long time, but now is the time to be thinking about what can be done to enhance inclusion for all.

Summary

This is a deeply complex and varied issue that you need to address as a teacher. There are a number of relatively simple changes that can be made to curriculum content, classroom management and organisation, environment and language that will have a positive impact on everyone, including the self-esteem of those who are questioning or trans as well as those who are cisgender, in terms of developing their respect, understanding and tolerance for the full range of identities. This is set to improve over time, but representation is key, and you have the opportunity to make significant headway here.

Policy summary

POLICY	KEY POINTS	IMPLICATIONS FOR SCHOOLS
EQUALITY ACT 2010	· IT IS ILLEGAL TO DISCRIMINATE AGAINST ANY OF THE NINE PROTECTED CHARACTERISTICS. FOR THIS ISSUE, THIS RELATES TO GENDER REASSIGNMENT AND SEX. ALL PROTECTED CHARACTERISTICS ARE EQUALLY WEIGHTED, AND TOLERANCE BETWEEN ALL GROUPS MUST BE EMPHASISED.	· PROMOTE COHESION, TOLERANCE AND RESPECT BETWEEN ALL GROUPS. · CHALLENGE AND TACKLE ANY INCIDENTS OF DISCRIMINATION, PARTICULARLY WHICH ARE TRANSPHOBIC IN NATURE. · EMBED MEANINGFUL TEACHING AND LEARNING OPPORTUNITIES RELATED TO GENDER EXPRESSION AND IDENTITIES ACROSS THE CURRICULUM.

POLICY	KEY POINTS	IMPLICATIONS FOR SCHOOLS
OFSTED: EXPLORING THE SCHOOL'S ACTIONS TO PREVENT AND TACKLE HOMOPHOBIC AND TRANSPHOBIC BULLYING (2013)	· INSPECTORS MAY TALK TO CHILDREN ABOUT THE FOLLOWING: - IF THEY EVER GET PICKED ON BY OTHER CHILDREN FOR NOT BEHAVING LIKE A 'TYPICAL GIRL' OR A 'TYPICAL BOY'; - IF THEY THINK IF THERE IS SOMEONE BORN A GIRL WHO WOULD RATHER BE A BOY OR BORN A BOY WHO WOULD LIKE TO BE A GIRL, THEY WOULD FEEL SAFE AT SCHOOL AND BE INCLUDED.	· USE THE QUESTIONS AND POINTS FROM THIS DOCUMENT TO ENSURE COMPLIANCE OF PROVISION AT ALL LEVELS. · ENSURE THAT THE CURRICULUM IS FULLY INCLUSIVE AND COVERS ALL OF THESE ISSUES. · RECORD-KEEPING OF ALL INCIDENTS IS ESSENTIAL AS IS SPECIFIC REFERENCE TO GENDER IDENTITY IN KEY POLICIES. · ENSURE THERE IS CLEAR EVIDENCE OF TRAINING UNDERTAKEN BY ALL STAFF AND CONSIDER THE IMPACT THIS HAS HAD.
	· SENIOR LEADERS AND DOCUMENTATION WILL BE SCRUTINISED IN TERMS OF HOW INCIDENTS OF TRANSPHOBIC LANGUAGE ARE RECORDED AND DEALT WITH. THE BULLYING AND SAFEGUARDING POLICIES AND EQUALITY OBJECTIVES WILL BE CHECKED TO ENSURE THEY ADDRESS GENDER IDENTITY. EVIDENCE OF TRAINING FOR STAFF WILL BE SOUGHT IN TERMS OF HOW TO TACKLE TRANSPHOBIC BULLYING, INCLUDING LANGUAGE. POLICIES WILL BE CHECKED TO ENSURE THAT THEY PROMOTE THE SAFETY OF ALL GROUPS, REGARDLESS OF GENDER IDENTITY. THE BULLYING, BEHAVIOUR AND EQUALITY POLICIES WILL BE CHECKED FOR SPECIFIC REFERENCE TO GENDER IDENTITY.	

POLICY	KEY POINTS	IMPLICATIONS FOR SCHOOLS
	· WITH GOVERNORS, OFSTED MAY EXPLORE: - HOW THE SCHOOL MEETS ITS STATUTORY DUTY TO PREVENT ALL FORMS OF PREJUDICE-BASED BULLYING, INCLUDING TRANSPHOBIA; - WHETHER THEY ARE AWARE OF ANY TRANSPHOBIC BULLYING OR LANGUAGE IN SCHOOL AND WHETHER INCIDENTS ARE FOLLOWED UP EFFECTIVELY; - HOW THEY ENSURE THAT GENDER EQUALITY IS COVERED WITHIN THE SCHOOL'S BEHAVIOUR GUIDELINES AND POLICIES.	
OFSTED HANDBOOK (2018)	· THIS HAS REMAINED UNCHANGED FOR A NUMBER OF YEARS. · OUTSTANDING: PUPILS WORK HARD WITH THE SCHOOL TO PREVENT ALL FORMS OF BULLYING, INCLUDING ONLINE AND PREJUDICE-BASED BULLYING. STAFF AND PUPILS DEAL EFFECTIVELY WITH THE VERY RARE INSTANCES OF BULLYING BEHAVIOUR AND/OR USE OF DEROGATORY OR AGGRESSIVE LANGUAGE.	· CONSIDER WHERE PRACTICE IN YOUR SCHOOL FALLS IN RELATION TO THESE CRITERIA AND THE ROBUSTNESS OF THE EVIDENCE YOU HAVE TO SUPPORT YOUR CLAIMS. ENGAGE WITH ALL STAKEHOLDERS, INCLUDING CHILDREN TO CHECK THE ACCURACY OF YOUR JUDGEMENTS.

POLICY	KEY POINTS	IMPLICATIONS FOR SCHOOLS
	• GOOD: TEACHERS AND OTHER ADULTS ARE QUICK TO TACKLE THE RARE USE OF DEROGATORY OR AGGRESSIVE LANGUAGE AND ALWAYS CHALLENGE STEREOTYPING. TEACHERS AND OTHER ADULTS PROMOTE CLEAR MESSAGES ABOUT THE IMPACT OF BULLYING AND PREJUDICED BEHAVIOUR ON PUPILS' WELL-BEING. PUPILS WORK WELL WITH THE SCHOOL TO TACKLE AND PREVENT THE RARE OCCURRENCES OF BULLYING. • INADEQUATE: INCIDENTS OF PREJUDICED AND DISCRIMINATORY BEHAVIOUR, BOTH DIRECT AND INDIRECT, ARE INFREQUENT. PUPILS HAVE LITTLE CONFIDENCE IN THE SCHOOL'S ABILITY TO TACKLE BULLYING SUCCESSFULLY.	
PREVENTING AND TACKLING BULLYING (DFE, 2017)	• THIS DOCUMENT NOTES THE SEVERE IMPACTS THAT MAY STEM FROM BULLYING AND DRAWS ON VARIOUS LEGISLATION; NOTING THE IMPORTANCE OF WORKING TOGETHER TO ACHIEVE THE BEST OUTCOMES FOR ALL.	• CONSIDER THE POINTS RAISED AND THE RESILIENCE AND EFFECTIVENESS OF YOUR SCHOOL POLICY AND PRACTICE IN ADDRESSING THESE. EXPLORE THE LINKS NOTED REGARDING LGBT AS APPROPRIATE.
LGBT ACTION PLAN (GEO, 2018)	• THINGS TO LOOK FOR STEMMING FROM THIS DOCUMENT WHICH IS BASED ON THE PRINCIPLE OF IMPROVING THE LIVES OF LGBT PEOPLE: - HBT BULLYING PROGRAMME TO BE INTRODUCED TO SCHOOLS.	• CONSIDER WHAT YOU ALREADY DO IN RELATION TO THESE AREAS AND IDENTIFY ACTIONS TO ENHANCE EXISTING PRACTICE.

POLICY	KEY POINTS	IMPLICATIONS FOR SCHOOLS
	- DEVELOPING AN UNDERSTANDING OF THE BEST WAYS TO SUPPORT SCHOOLS TO TACKLE HBT BULLYING AND HOW TO CONTINUE THIS IN A SUSTAINED MANNER THROUGH THE CURRICULUM. - UPDATES TO THE CROWN PROSECUTION SERVICE LGBT HATE CRIMES PACK FOR SCHOOLS (FOR KEY STAGES 3 AND 4, BUT THESE COULD PROVIDE FOOD FOR THOUGHT FOR EARLIER PHASES). - DFE UPDATED GUIDANCE RELATED TO HOW SCHOOLS CAN APPLY THE EQUALITY ACT OF 2010. - LGBT TEACHERS TO BE SUPPORTED TO BE THEMSELVES AT WORK.	
GENDER SEPARATION IN MIXED SCHOOLS: NON-STATUTORY GUIDANCE (DFE, JUNE 2018)	· NOTES THAT SCHOOLS SHOULD NOT SEPARATE BY SEX (OR ANY OTHER PROTECTED CHARACTERISTIC). THE ONLY EXCEPTIONS TO THIS ARE: - POSITIVE ACTION: SEPARATION BY SEX CAN BE JUSTIFIED IF GIRLS OR BOYS SUFFER A DISADVANTAGE CONNECTED TO THEIR SEX; GIRLS OR BOYS HAVE NEEDS THAT ARE DIFFERENT TO THE NEEDS OF THE OTHER SEX; OR PARTICIPATION IN AN ACTIVITY BY GIRLS OR BOYS IS DISPROPORTIONATELY LOW.	· CONSIDER WHERE GENDER SEPARATION OCCURS, IF AT ALL, IN YOUR SCHOOL AND ENSURE THAT YOU CAN JUSTIFY THIS IN THE CONTEXT OF THE LEGAL REQUIREMENTS EXEMPLIFIED IN THIS DOCUMENT, BASED ON THE 2010 EQUALITY ACT. · IF ALLOWED GROUPS ARE SEPARATED BY SEX, YOU MUST ENSURE THAT BOTH TEAMS HAVE EQUAL OPPORTUNITIES AND EQUAL QUALITY RESOURCES.

GENDER AND IDENTITY

POLICY	KEY POINTS	IMPLICATIONS FOR SCHOOLS
	- COMPETITIVE SPORT: THIS RELATES TO COMPETITIVE SPORTS WHERE THE PHYSICAL STRENGTH, STAMINA OR PHYSIQUE OF THE AVERAGE GIRL OR BOY WOULD PUT HER OR HIM AT A DISADVANTAGE IN A COMPETITION WITH THE AVERAGE BOY OR GIRL. THERE SHOULD, HOWEVER, STILL BE EQUAL OPPORTUNITIES FOR ALL TO PARTICIPATE IN COMPARABLE SPORTING ACTIVITIES.	
	- IF THERE WERE SEPARATE TEAMS FOR DIFFERENT SEXES, IT WOULD BE UNLAWFUL FOR THE SCHOOL TO PROVIDE ONE SEX'S TEAM WITH BETTER EQUIPMENT THAN THE OTHER.	

❖ Critical questions

1. How well do you feel you understand the range of gender expressions and identities?

2. How effectively do you incorporate a range of gender identities into your teaching across the curriculum?

3. What will you do as a result of this chapter to enhance the visibility of a range of gender identities within your classroom, school and curriculum?

4. Do you promote or perpetuate gender stereotypes? How will you address these?

5. What actions will you take to reinforce your acceptance and celebration of the full range of gender identities that may/do exist in your school?

6. What do you do to challenge stereotypes and how effective has this been?

7. How effectively does your school emphasise that transphobia is unacceptable? What part have you played in this? How might this be further enhanced in your setting?

8. What training have you had about issues around gender and identity? What are the training needs within your school and who should be involved?

9. If you separate children by sex or gender for any activity, are you confident that this has not led to children suffering any detriment as a result of their sex or gender?

10. What opportunities might you give to children to develop a positive sense of self-worth and identity to reinforce the importance of respecting and celebrating a range of identities?

11. How else can you group children, apart from by gender?

12. What action(s) will you take to address transphobic actions or language?

13. Which aspects of school policy and practice may need to be reconsidered to improve outcomes and experiences for trans children?

14. Which resources would enhance your practice, how might these be used and how will you disseminate good practice to colleagues?

15. Do your school's equality, behaviour and bullying policies make specific reference to gender identity?

further reading and resources

Gendered Intelligence (http://genderedintelligence.co.uk)	An organisation that works with young people under 21 to increase understanding about gender diversity.
Mermaids (www.mermaidsuk.org.uk)	A website that provides support for children, young people and their families who are dealing with gender issues.
Gender Identity Research and Education Society (www.gires.org.uk)	An organisation that promotes education about gender identity to improve the lives of those of all identities. The website contains a range of educational resources to support understanding.
Educate & Celebrate (www.educateandcelebrate.org)	A range of resources covering the range of LGBT+ issues to support teaching at all stages.

Stonewall (www.stonewall.org.uk)	A range of resources and training opportunities concerning the full range of LGBT+ issues, including gender identity.
Kids' Guide to Gender (www. kidsguidetogender.com)	This website goes alongside the book, ***Who Are You? The Kid****'s Guide to Gender Identity*, by Brook Pessin-Whedbee. This website provides classroom resources, including lesson plans, videos and story ideas. A particularly powerful story about gender identity suggested here is *Red: A Crayon's Story* by Michael Hall. The ideas provide a progressive structure to support children's developing understanding.
Brooks, B (2018) *Stories for Boys Who Dare to Be Different: True Tales of Amazing Boys Who Changed the World Without Killing Dragons*, London: Quercus; and Brooks, B (2018) *Stories for Kids Who Dare to Be Different: True Tales of Boys and Girls Who Stood Up and Stood Out*, London: Quercus.	Short stories about real people who have challenged stereotypical behaviour and made an impact on the world.
Atkinson, C J (2017) *Can I Tell You About Gender Diversity?* London: Jessica Kingsley Publishers.	A book that explains issues around gender diversity in accessible language and a child-friendly format.
Carlile, A and Barnes, E (2018) *How to Transform Your School into an LGBT+ Friendly Place*, London: Jessica Kingsley Publishers.	A practical guide to best practice in relation to LGBT+ friendly schools.
Pop 'n' Olly (www.popnolly.com)	A website aimed at children that covers a range of LGBT+ issues. There are a number of useful video resources related to gender, including: *Gender Diversity Explained for Children, The Gender Unicorn* and *Little Red Riding Dude* (a gender non-conforming fairy tale).

References

Branson, L B (2016) The Gender Binary Explained through Toys [Online Video]. 28 June. [online] Available at: www.buzzfeed.com/bransonlb/the-gender-binary-explained-through-toys (accessed 10 April 2019).

Brooks, B (2018) *Stories for Kids Who Dare to Be Different: True Tales of Boys and Girls Who Stood Up and Stood Out*. London: Quercus.

Department for Education (2018) *Gender Separation in Mixed Schools: Non-Statutory Guidance*. London: DfE.

Educational Action Challenging Homophobia (2016) What Is Gender? (Inspiring Equality in Education). [online] Available at: www.youtube.com/watch?v=qlYtj0sf6ec (accessed 10 April 2019).

Government Equalities Office (2018a) *LGBT Action Plan: Improving the Lives of Lesbian, Gay, Bisexual and Transgender People*. London: GEO.

Government Equalities Office (2018b) Reform of the Gender Recognition Act 2004. [online] Available at: www.gov.uk/government/consultations/reform-of-the-gender-recognition-act-2004 (accessed 10 April 2019).

It Gets Better Project (2018) LGBTQ+ Glossary. [online] Available at: https://itgetsbetter.org/lesson/glossary/ (accessed 10 April 2019).

Stein, R (2018) Why Everyone Should Watch Butterfly. [online] Available at: www.stonewall.org.uk/our-work/blog/why-everyone-should-watch-butterfly (accessed 10 April 2019).

Stonewall (2017a) School Report. [online] Available at: www.stonewall.org.uk/school-report-2017 (accessed 10 April 2019).

Stonewall (2017b) A Vision for Change. [online] Available at: www.stonewall.org.uk/system/files/a_vision_for_change.pdf (accessed 10 April 2019).

Stonewall (2018) Gender Recognition Act. [online] Available at: www.stonewall.org.uk/gender-recognition-act (accessed 10 April 2019).

Tate, G (2018) Butterfly Review: A Well-Intended Pushback Against Lazy Prejudice. [online] Available at: www.telegraph.co.uk/tv/2018/10/14/butterfly-review-well-intended-pushback-against-lazy-prejudice/ (accessed 10 April 2019).

7. TACKLING PREJUDICE-BASED BULLYING: HOMOPHOBIA AND BIPHOBIA

Key issues

Prejudice-based bullying, sadly, is nothing new, and, while legislation since the late 1960s has shown significant and positive progress in gay rights, it remains an area about which many teachers, parents and carers feel trepidation, and, as a result, they are not fully at ease in addressing the issues. As someone working with primary-aged children, you have a legal responsibility to ensure that issues surrounding different types of family, relationships and prejudice-based bullying are effectively tackled across the whole curriculum in age-appropriate ways. Statistics from the 2014 *Teachers' Report* by Stonewall showed that 70 per cent of primary-school teachers heard children using homophobic language in their schools. While being willing to tackle it, they lacked the confidence to do so. This chapter focuses on issues around sexuality and not gender. While there are common themes affecting all of these groups, it is important to note the distinctions between groups so we do not ignore specific aspects of the experiences of each group.

What is homophobic language?

It is essential, first, to be clear that the use of words such as *lesbian*, *gay* and *bisexual* in the correct context is totally acceptable and should be encouraged as part of everyday vocabulary. When it is used with negative connotations, such as, 'My whiteboard pen has run out, it's so gay!', however, this is absolutely unacceptable, and you must challenge this each and every time that you hear it. Initially, this can be quite intensive, but consistency is the key to eliminating inappropriate and potentially offensive upsetting use of the language. It is not uncommon to hear adults shushing a child if they use the term *gay*, but you need to be very careful here. If talking about someone who is gay, this is fine. Suggesting that children should not be using 'that sort of word' implies inferiority of the said label. As a teacher, you should be modelling the correct use of terminology, and this should become a usual part of your practice. I always find the term 'usualising' (Sanders, cited by Barnes and Carlile, 2018, p 134) helpful here as this, '*makes the range of people's characteristics something people come into contact with on an every-day basis, thus, making them so usual as not to become taboo, or subject to ridicule or bullying.*'

THE DANGERS OF DISMISSAL

Using the language in a (potentially) derogatory manner certainly does not mean that a person is homophobic or biphobic. This said, casual use of the word *gay* as a substitute for alternatives such as dismal, dull, insipid, poor, pitiful, silly or idiotic does need to be challenged each time it is heard by any member of the school community, including children, or you end up with a very unhelpful, potentially unintentional, acceptance. This acceptance can lead to attitudes of intolerance, prejudice and bullying in later life and broader society. There is a strong Ofsted focus on preparing children for life in modern Britain. You should consider how ignoring such language use serves to do this. Failure to challenge this blasé misuse of language can result in children deeming it to be acceptable. In your school, there should be a clear policy in place that includes transphobia (tackled in Chapter 6), biphobia and homophobia.

POTENTIAL IMPACT ON ALL GROUPS

It is not just people who identify as L, G or B who may be affected by inappropriate use of language. You could challenge what young children know about their sexuality, but, regardless of this, within any class, there will be a diversity of family backgrounds, including same-sex parents. When children begin school, their experience of diversity may be limited, and they may well see their family as 'normal.' Once children start to be exposed to a breadth of family constitutions, this can lead to questioning, which is why you need to equip children with the attitudes and values that enable them to acknowledge and celebrate the very diverse nature of our society. This will go a significant way to ensuring that everyone feels recognised, valued and respected. Open, routine conversations about diversity through an integrated curriculum will help to reduce the ignorance and tackle the lack of accurate information which children may receive and therefore impede (or eliminate) the growth of prejudiced attitudes, perspectives and actions. It is all too easy to dismiss the careless or inappropriate use of language as 'banter', but you need to consider the impact it has on recipients.

POTENTIAL LONGER TERM IMPACTS

Linked to this in the longer term is the potential restriction on young people's confidence in coming out. A key point made by Gareth Thomas in his autobiography *Proud* emphasises the deep-rooted impact inappropriate use of language can have, '*I became more introverted every time I'd hear the word "gay", or a similar term used in a derogatory fashion. I would retreat deeper into myself*' (Thomas, 2014, p 63). No one should feel so uncomfortable about being themselves, and it is by addressing prejudiced use of language and challenging the ludicrous nature of some statements, such as, '*He's a … bender, can't catch a ball to save his life*' (Thomas, 2014, p 63) that you can make a positive difference for all children. From the early years, there is a need to make everyone feel accepted in society and equip everyone with the experience and understanding of diversity to realise what should be a simple and desirable goal. Again, challenge is the key to moving things on and developing a safer society in which heteronormativity (Barnes and Carlile, 2018) is challenged so as to more accurately reflect societal diversity.

CONSIDERING THE WHOLE SCHOOL ENVIRONMENT

You will need to consider the contexts in which such language may be used. In my experience, this will often not be in the classroom as children will be aware of the behavioural expectations in this context. It is in places such as the playground where you may well hear inappropriate use of the language; this may be deliberate or unintentional. Regardless, it needs to be tackled immediately, so you need to reflect upon the confidence of all members of staff, not just teachers, but lunchtime supervisors, administrative staff and so on. If they are unaware and let things go, not only does this give the children a message about acceptability, but it also negates all of the positive work that should be happening in the classroom across the curriculum.

What exactly is homophobic and biphobic bullying?

As you have already seen, there is potential for homophobic language to be used unintentionally and unwittingly, but it is essential for you to have a clear definition of what homophobic bullying is. This is important, not least because sometimes children and their parents will use the term 'bullying' in a broad and often inaccurate sense. Hall (2016, p 6) defines homophobic bullying as:

bullying that is based on prejudice or negative attitudes, beliefs or views about lesbian, gay or bisexual people … may be targeted at pupils who are or who are perceived to be L, G or B. It can also suggest that someone or something is less worthy because they are L, G or B … is often targeted at pupils who have L, G or B family members and pupils who do not conform to gender stereotypes or are seen to be 'different' in some way.

Biphobia is included in the above definition, but it is important to note that this is specific to bisexual people. You should also consider if this 'bullying' is something of which children are aware, ie, are they doing this intentionally, knowing that they are upsetting the recipient? Is it something that is repeated over time? Taking into consideration the most recent version of *Preventing and Tackling Bullying* (DfE, 2017, p 8), it is pertinent to note that bullying is something that is, '*repeated over time . . . intentionally hurts another individual or group either physically or emotionally.*' With education and usualising the use of the language, the incidents of bullying should be significantly reduced. Chapter 3 talks about issues around online safety, and it should be noted here that online homophobic or biphobic bullying remains a growing area of concern, not least because it is inescapable. Preparing children through the regular and routine use of language and enhancing their confidence to tackle and challenge the abuse will inevitably have a positive impact in relation to potential online issues.

As with any form of bullying, the potential to negatively impact an individual's confidence and sense of self-worth is immense. Charlesworth (2015) talks about this being the least reported form of bullying. A number of reasons are suggested for this, including:

- fears about coming out;
- dismissing it as badinage;
- the lack of confidence in schools related to how homophobic bullying will be responded to.

The points discussed thus far reinforce how pivotal you and the school's policy in action are to enabling children to report any form of bullying, including that which is homophobic or biphobic.

LGB(T) teachers

Teachers often grapple with whether to divulge information about their relationships to their colleagues and their pupils. Often there is a level of reticence or reluctance to 'come out' in the workplace. If you are L, G or B, you should feel comfortable and confident to come out about your relationship. As with any relationship, this does not mean giving unnecessary intimate detail but acknowledging and celebrating your relationship. I recall hearing my teachers talking about their (heterosexual) partners but never about any same-sex partners. This can give children a skewed sense of the world and again reinforce that idea of heteronormativity. Barnes and Carlile (2018, p 24) make a point that will make you think carefully about your stance here: '*If there is resistance to the idea of teachers being out, ask straight (heterosexual) colleagues what they do if they bump into a student on the bus or in the supermarket. Do they suddenly need to drop their partner's hand?*' So far, this chapter has mainly talked about issues from a child's perspective, but you also need to consider the feeling of belonging for LGBT colleagues and their comfort in the workplace. Surely, if you are trying to promote these positive values in children, you must model them in every possible way to the children in your school. This point is also at the heart of the government's LGBT Action Plan (GEO, 2018).

Progress in legislation?

LEGALISATION AND SECTION 28

The 1967 legalisation of homosexuality in England and Wales was a very positive step forward. However, nearly 20 years later a piece of legislation was introduced that had long-lasting ramifications. Section 28 of the Local Government Act 1988 codified in law that homosexuality should not be promoted as acceptable by the local authority. It also referred to homosexual relationships as '*pretended family units*' (HM Government, 1988). Section 28 was the law until 2003, so since then it has been acceptable to talk about gay, lesbian and bisexual people and relationships in schools, but it is debatable as to how well understood this is on a practical level. The word 'promote' continues to be a source of debate, with people having concerns about whether talking about something promotes it. Barnes and Carlile (2018) note the concerns of educators who question if talking about (promoting) homosexuality will make their pupils gay. A comparative question identified is: '*When we study the Paralympics are we promoting disabilities?*' (Barnes and Carlile, 2018, p 29). The key thing for you to remember, linked to Part Two of the Teachers' Standards (DfE, 2011), is that you are simply recognising and celebrating the diversity that exists within society, treating everyone with dignity and respect so as to prepare them for life in modern Britain. With such contentious issues very much at the fore during these fifteen years, the legacy has lived on, and you are in a position now to make significant shifts in practice to put this outdated law to bed once and for all.

THE REPEAL OF SECTION 28 AND BEYOND

From 2003, there has been some good progress, but the impact is relatively slow in coming through. Following the repeal of Section 28, we saw the introduction of LGBT History Month, which is celebrated every February. Is this something that you mark in your school? It often seems that it is seen that this is more appropriate for secondary schools and colleges, but you need to consider what may be holding primary schools back.

Civil partnerships were introduced in 2004, showing progress in terms of formally acknowledging gay relationships. Often, parents and carers are cited as a reason for being tentative around these issues, but you need to consider the acceptability of this stance as well as the potential negative impact on the esteem of those parents and carers who live in same-sex relationships. I would argue that the most powerful legislation in recent years is the Equality Act of 2010 which states that it is against the law to discriminate against anyone in relation to any of the nine identified protected characteristics, of which sexual orientation is one. Surely overlooking gay relationships could be deemed to be showing discrimination, and Charlesworth (2015, p 66) argues that, '*Silence can send the loudest message about the value placed on lesbian, gay and bisexual identities.*' This is something that you should consider as part of your reflection about your curriculum design, content and delivery. I suppose we return to the notion of promotion here again – by celebrating

LGBT History Month, are you 'promoting' being gay? No, you are simply preparing children for life where they are legally required to respect and tolerate diversity.

OFSTED

Stemming from the Equality Act of 2010, Ofsted, in 2013, introduced a key change to their criteria and produced a document entitled, *Exploring the School's Actions to Prevent and Tackle Homophobic and Transphobic Bullying*. This has led to a clear focus on how schools should proactively tackle these issues through all aspects of their work. The critical questions at the end of this chapter will help you to ensure strong practice related to current Ofsted (2018) requirements.

Sometimes you will hear people talking about how it is not appropriate for young children to know about same-sex relationships, but children will see these all around them as well as the issues being talked about in the media. You need to feel comfortable to talk about these issues with children and with parents and carers so as to prepare them to lead tolerant and respectful lives that celebrate societal diversity. The debates will continue, and we will see more countries legalising same-sex marriage (made legal in the UK in 2013), debates around the issue of pardoning gay men for past convictions (pre-1967), the legalisation of gay sex as passed in India in September 2018 and issues concerned with faith.

RAISING THE PROFILE AND AWARENESS

In 2017, the Crown Prosecution Service reported rising volumes of hate crime being reported to the police. As part of their response, it was stated that online and offline crimes would be treated equally seriously by the authorities. Children need to be aware of the issue of hate crime and the importance of reporting it. The Crown Prosecution Service has been using social media to encourage people to come forward (#HateCrimeMatters), and it is through your teaching that you can give children the confidence and language to recognise and report these crimes when they occur.

July 2018 saw the publication of the LGBT Action Plan by the GEO (2018, p 1). This celebrates the progress to date in ensuring equality for LGBT+ people but notes there is still a long way to go, emphasising that:

One statistic alone speaks volumes. Two-thirds of respondents said they had avoided holding their same-sex partner's hand in public for fear of a negative reaction. Holding hands with someone you love should be one of the simplest things in the world; not a source of fear or hesitation.

THE CURRICULUM

This reinforces the need to usualise this issue as part of everyday life throughout the primary curriculum (see the example boxes below). The issue of identity, and recognition of all identities, in a safe and supported environment is at the heart of this document and must underpin all that you do in the classroom. Significant investment is being made by the GEO, and sustainability through the school curriculum and policies is central to achieving success in homophobic, biphobic and transphobic bullying. Another element that is pertinent to note is the planned update to guidance about how schools should apply the Equality Act (2010). Hate crime has been a significant agenda item in recent years, and further guidance for educational institutions is planned. Linked with Part Two of the Teachers' Standards (DfE, 2011), you have a pivotal role in ensuring that children understand the rule of law. There will continue to be developments in legislation that will impact on your role and continue to enhance the levels of acceptance and safety for all children and young people, whatever their identity.

Good practice example

KEY STAGE 1 ENGLISH
FAIRY STORIES AND TRADITIONAL TALES

The principle here could be adapted to any age, using the Stonewall or Educate & Celebrate book lists. Instead of the usual texts, use a story such as 'The Prince and the Frog' by Olly Pike.

- Share and enjoy the story.
- Draw out the features of the genre.
- Discuss issues around being in a respectful and loving relationship, being kind to others and celebrate the diversity and equality.
- When the children write their story, celebrate the range of types of relationship their stories portray.

KEY STAGE 2 HISTORY

Study an aspect or theme in British history that extends pupils' chronological knowledge beyond 1066; eg, a significant turning point in British history. There is ample scope to include people who are LGB in Key Stage 1 units about significant individuals. For example, you may explore Tim Peake and use Sally Ride to compare and contrast. Both were astronauts, but there is opportunity to talk about gender stereotyping and the hidden nature of Ride's lesbian relationship.

ALAN TURING AND THE BREAKING OF THE ENIGMA CODE

- Engage the children in historical enquiry about the events leading up to the breaking of the Enigma Code through asking and answering questions, drawing upon a range of sources and making judgements by sifting through evidence.

- Look at interpretations of Alan Turing as a key person here and the way he was persecuted as a result of his sexuality and the tragic outcome this had. What views were expressed and why?

- Use a story about Turing, such as the one in the book *Stories for Boys Who Dare to Be Different* by Ben Brooks to draw out key points related to Turing's life. Explore how his treatment by society resulting from his sexuality was unacceptable.

- Debate issues around the pardoning of gay men through what is known informally as the 'Turing Law.'

Faith

Faith is often cited as a concern teachers have about teaching an LGBT+ inclusive curriculum. While this is an understandable issue, it certainly should not be a barrier, or indeed an excuse, to not address the issues. There is often (mis)interpretation of religious texts that can lead to prejudiced attitudes and discrimination coming through, but regardless of people's religious or cultural beliefs, it must be noted that no religion condones any form of bullying or harassment. September 2018 saw an announcement by Chief Rabbi Ephraim Mirvis, stating that Orthodox Jewish schools need to be LGBT+ inclusive as failure to do so can lead to devastating consequences, including suicide. Documents such as, *The Wellbeing of LGBT+ Pupils: A Guide for Orthodox Jewish Schools*, *Valuing All God's Children: Guidance for Church of England Schools on Challenging Homophobic, Biphobic and Transphobic Bullying* and organisations such as Imaan (an LGBTQ Muslim charity) show the strides being taken by various faith communities to ensure that all children feel loved, valued and safe regardless of any aspect of their identity. These are also very helpful documents to deal with any faith-based prejudice or resistance in a supportive confident and respectful manner.

Curriculum and resources

There are constantly issues to consider regarding the curriculum and its inclusivity; this is nothing new. Having said this, it is essential that you look carefully at the resources you use in terms of how they recognise and celebrate the full range of families. This should not be onerous. Simple things include considering the characters you explore through your teaching of history. Does this include LGB people? Story is notably a highly effective way of alerting children to diversity and opening up conversations to encourage the usualisation of a wide range of identities and relationships. There are a wide range of resources already out there, and these continue to grow. Some key resources are noted at the end of the chapter, but it is worth taking time to review and consider texts identified by Educate & Celebrate, Stonewall and the No Outsiders resources. This is another one of those things that is best integrated throughout the curriculum rather than doing a distinct unit about gay relationships, in the same way as you have seen SMSC interwoven throughout the curriculum. Through regular integration and display, you are breaking down any stigma and making it a usual part of everyday life; it is no big deal!

Summary

Tackling homophobia and biphobia is essential in promoting the acceptance and respect that is needed towards everyone in our diverse society. This is not about sexualising children, but acknowledging the diverse range of relationships and family types that exist. The visibility of such family diversity should be a usual part of everyday practice throughout the curriculum so that it does not become a source of fear or taboo. You have a responsibility to celebrate diversity in all its forms and to challenge inappropriate use of language each and every time it is heard. Stories are a fantastic medium through which to support your work in this area and there are a growing number of stories being published that feature diversity. Everyone should be allowed to feel comfortable with their identity and not have to hide any aspect of this through fear. With consistent messages, this can be achieved.

Policy summary

POLICY	KEY POINTS	IMPLICATIONS FOR SCHOOLS
EQUALITY ACT 2010	· IT IS ILLEGAL TO DISCRIMINATE AGAINST ANY OF THE NINE PROTECTED CHARACTERISTICS. FOR THIS ISSUE, THIS COULD INCLUDE: MARRIAGE AND CIVIL PARTNERSHIP AND SEXUAL ORIENTATION. ALL PROTECTED CHARACTERISTICS ARE EQUALLY WEIGHTED, AND TOLERANCE BETWEEN THE DIFFERENT GROUPS MUST BE EMPHASISED.	· PROMOTE COHESION, TOLERANCE AND RESPECT BETWEEN ALL GROUPS. · CHALLENGE AND TACKLE ANY INCIDENTS OF DISCRIMINATION. · INCORPORATE MEANINGFUL TEACHING AND LEARNING OPPORTUNITIES AROUND THE ISSUES.
OFSTED: EXPLORING THE SCHOOL'S ACTIONS TO PREVENT AND TACKLE HOMOPHOBIC AND TRANSPHOBIC BULLYING (2013)	· THIS ISSUE IS A KEY FOCUS FOR OFSTED INSPECTIONS. THE DOCUMENT (p 3) STATES THAT INSPECTORS MAY TALK ABOUT THE FOLLOWING WITH CHILDREN: - IF PUPILS EVER HEAR ANYONE USE THE WORD 'GAY' WHEN DESCRIBING SOMETHING, OR WHETHER THEY HAVE BEEN TOLD BY TEACHERS THAT USING THE WORD 'GAY', TO MEAN SOMETHING IS RUBBISH, IS WRONG, SCARY OR UNPLEASANT AND WHY IT IS WRONG. - IF PUPILS EVER GET PICKED ON BY OTHER CHILDREN FOR NOT BEHAVING LIKE A 'TYPICAL GIRL' OR A 'TYPICAL BOY.'	· USE THE QUESTIONS AND POINTS FROM THE DOCUMENT TO ENSURE THE COMPLIANCE OF PROVISION AT ALL LEVELS. · ENSURE THAT THE CURRICULUM IS INCLUSIVE AND FULLY COVERS THESE ISSUES. · RECORD-KEEPING OF ALL INCIDENTS IS ESSENTIAL AS IS SPECIFIC REFERENCE TO SEXUALITY IN KEY POLICIES. · ENSURE THAT THERE IS CLEAR EVIDENCE OF TRAINING FOR ALL STAFF AND CONSIDER THE IMPACT THIS HAS HAD.

POLICY	KEY POINTS	IMPLICATIONS FOR SCHOOLS
	- IF PUPILS HAVE HAD ANY LESSONS ABOUT DIFFERENT TYPES OF FAMILIES (SINGLE PARENT, LIVING WITH GRANDPARENTS, HAVING STEP-PARENTS, HAVING TWO MUMS OR TWO DADS).	
	• SENIOR LEADERS AND DOCUMENTATION WILL BE SCRUTINISED IN TERMS OF HOW ANY INCIDENTS OF HOMOPHOBIC LANGUAGE ARE RECORDED AND DEALT WITH. THE BULLYING AND SAFEGUARDING POLICIES WILL BE CHECKED TO ENSURE REFERENCE TO SEXUALITY. EVIDENCE OF TRAINING FOR STAFF IN TACKLING HOMOPHOBIC LANGUAGE WILL BE EXPLORED. OFSTED WILL ALSO ENSURE THAT POLICIES REFER TO CARERS AS WELL AS PARENTS AND HOW LGB FAMILIES ARE BEING SUPPORTED BY THE SCHOOL. • WITH GOVERNORS, OFSTED MAY EXPLORE (p 4): *- HOW THE SCHOOL MEETS ITS STATUTORY DUTY TO PREVENT ALL FORMS OF PREJUDICE-BASED BULLYING, INCLUDING HOMOPHOBIA* *- WHETHER THEY ARE AWARE OF ANY HOMOPHOBIC BULLYING OR LANGUAGE IN SCHOOL AND WHETHER INCIDENTS ARE FOLLOWED UP EFFECTIVELY*	

POLICY	KEY POINTS	IMPLICATIONS FOR SCHOOLS
	- HOW THEY ENSURE THAT SEXUALITY IS COVERED WITHIN THE SCHOOL'S BEHAVIOUR GUIDELINES AND POLICIES.	
OFSTED HANDBOOK (2018)	• THIS HAS REMAINED UNCHANGED FOR A NUMBER OF YEARS. • OUTSTANDING: PUPILS WORK HARD WITH THE SCHOOL TO PREVENT ALL FORMS OF BULLYING, INCLUDING ONLINE AND PREJUDICE-BASED BULLYING. STAFF AND PUPILS DEAL EFFECTIVELY WITH THE VERY RARE INSTANCES OF BULLYING BEHAVIOUR OR USE OF DEROGATORY OR AGGRESSIVE LANGUAGE.	• CONSIDER WHERE PRACTICE IN YOUR SCHOOL FALLS IN RELATION TO THE CRITERIA AND THE ROBUSTNESS OF THE EVIDENCE YOU HAVE TO SUPPORT YOUR CLAIMS. • ENGAGE WITH ALL STAKEHOLDERS, INCLUDING CHILDREN TO CHECK THE ACCURACY OF YOUR JUDGEMENTS.
	• GOOD: TEACHERS AND OTHER ADULTS ARE QUICK TO TACKLE THE RARE USE OF DEROGATORY OR AGGRESSIVE LANGUAGE AND ALWAYS CHALLENGE STEREOTYPING. TEACHERS AND OTHER ADULTS PROMOTE CLEAR MESSAGES ABOUT THE IMPACT OF BULLYING AND PREJUDICED BEHAVIOUR ON PUPILS' WELL-BEING. PUPILS WORK WELL WITH THE SCHOOL TO TACKLE AND PREVENT THE RARE OCCURRENCES OF BULLYING.	

POLICY	KEY POINTS	IMPLICATIONS FOR SCHOOLS
	· INADEQUATE: INCIDENTS OF PREJUDICED AND DISCRIMINATORY BEHAVIOUR, BOTH DIRECT AND INDIRECT ARE INFREQUENT. PUPILS HAVE LITTLE CONFIDENCE IN THE SCHOOL'S ABILITY TO TACKLE BULLYING SUCCESSFULLY.	
PREVENTING AND TACKLING BULLYING (DFE, 2017)	· THIS DOCUMENT NOTES THE SEVERE IMPACTS THAT MAY STEM FROM BULLYING AND DRAWS ON VARIOUS LEGISLATION; NOTING THE IMPORTANCE OF WORKING TOGETHER TO ACHIEVE THE BEST OUTCOMES FOR ALL.	· CONSIDER THE POINTS RAISED AND THE RESILIENCE AND EFFECTIVENESS OF YOUR SCHOOL POLICY AND PRACTICE IN ADDRESSING THESE. · EXPLORE THE LINKS NOTED REGARDING LGBT AS APPROPRIATE.
LGBT ACTION PLAN (GEO, 2018)	· THINGS TO LOOK FOR STEMMING FROM THIS DOCUMENT WHICH IS BASED ON THE PRINCIPLE OF IMPROVING THE LIVES OF LGBT PEOPLE: - HBT BULLYING PROGRAMME TO BE INTRODUCED TO SCHOOLS. - DEVELOPING AN UNDERSTANDING OF THE BEST WAYS TO SUPPORT SCHOOLS TO TACKLE HBT BULLYING AND HOW TO CONTINUE THIS IN A SUSTAINED MANNER THROUGH THE CURRICULUM.	· CONSIDER WHAT YOU ALREADY DO IN RELATION TO THESE AREAS AND IDENTIFY ACTIONS TO ENHANCE EXISTING PRACTICE.

POLICY	KEY POINTS	IMPLICATIONS FOR SCHOOLS
	- UPDATES TO THE CROWN PROSECUTION SERVICE LGBT HATE CRIMES PACK FOR SCHOOLS (FOR KEY STAGES 3 AND 4, BUT THESE COULD PROVIDE FOOD FOR THOUGHT FOR EARLY PHASES). · DFE UPDATED GUIDANCE RELATED TO HOW SCHOOLS CAN APPLY THE EQUALITY ACT OF 2010. - LGBT TEACHERS TO BE SUPPORTED TO BE THEMSELVES AT WORK.	

❖ Critical questions

1. How confident do you feel in fulfilling your statutory duties in terms of tackling prejudice-based bullying? What are any inhibiting factors and how might you overcome these?

2. Have all staff been trained in how to tackle the inappropriate use of language and how confident do they feel in doing this? Is there evidence that this is working based on how effectively incidents are reported and dealt with?

3. How inclusive is your curriculum? How might this be further enhanced so as to usualise the various family types? Are there any resource implications? What amendments could be made to your current practice?

4. Have you ever ignored inappropriate use of language by children (or colleagues)? Why was this? What will you do now to make challenge a regular part of your practice?

5. Do you routinely model appropriate use of the language to children?

6. Does your school have a clear statement in behaviour and bullying policies about homophobic and biphobic bullying and language? How effectively are these implemented? What needs to be done to enhance practice in this area?

7. Do you understand the diversity of family types in your class? How do you ensure that this is reflected in all elements of your practice?

8. Consider examples of derogatory language use that you have heard. Reflect on why it was so important to challenge each of these.

9. How do your school and classroom environment and resources reflect societal diversity?

10. How well prepared are your pupils to recognise and deal with homophobic or biphobic bullying/language?

11. Are LGBT staff encouraged to discuss and celebrate their relationships in school?

12. Is there any evidence of a negative legacy of Section 28 in your school? What might you do to help overcome this?

13. To what extent do you celebrate events such as LGBT History Month in your school? Are there any inhibiting factors and what might overcome these?

14. How effectively is the Equality Act 2010 understood and implemented in your school? Consider this in relation to children, parents, carers and staff.

15. To what extent is the issue invisible or overlooked in your school or class?

16. Where does your school or classroom practice fall in relation to the current Ofsted criteria related to the issue? How do you know? What evidence do you have to support your assessment? How could this be enhanced? What are the enabling and inhibiting factors?

17. How might you use resources from various faith organisations to address issues concerning religion or faith with children, parents, carers and staff?

18. How does your school communicate and work with parents and carers on this issue? What has the impact of this work been? What opportunities are there to enhance this?

further reading and resources

Letterbox Library (www.equalitiesprimary.com)	Resources to support the teaching of the Equality Act.
LGBT History Month (http://lgbthistorymonth.org.uk)	Information and resources about LGBT History Month (celebrated each February).

The Classroom (http://the-classroom.org.uk)	A wide range of up-to-date resources to support schools in meeting their legal duties in relation to the latest policy.
Stonewall (www.stonewall.org.uk and www.stonewall.org.uk/our-work/education-resources)	There is a wide range of resources in the 'Our Work' and 'Education Resources' section for all phases, including primary.
Educate & Celebrate (www.educateandcelebrate.org)	A range of resources, including suggested books and lesson plans for early years and primary.
Pop 'n' Olly (www.popnolly.com)	A website based around LGBT+ and equality education for children, parents, carers and teachers.
EACH (https://each.education/)	A range of issues for all phases, including primary.
PSHE [Personal, Social, Health and Economic] Association (www.pshe-association.org.uk/content/government-equalities-office-anti-homophobic)	Resources supporting the GEO anti-homophobic, biphobic and transphobic bullying project. This website includes links to: Stonewall, Barnardo's, LGBT Consortium, Learn Equality: Live Equal, Rainbow Flag Award and Metro Charity. Each site contains a range of downloadable materials.

References

Barnes, E and Carlile, A (2018) *How to Transform Your School into an LGBT+ Friendly Place*. London: Jessica Kingsley.

Charlesworth, J (2015) *That's So Gay! Challenging Homophobic Bullying*. London: Jessica Kingsley.

Department for Education (2011) *Teachers' Standards*. London: DfE.

Department for Education (2017) *Preventing and Tackling Bullying*. London: DfE.

Government Equalities Office (2018) *LGBT Action Plan*. London: GEO.

HM Government (1988) Local Government Act 1988 Section 28. [online] Available at: www.legislation.gov.uk/ukpga/1988/9/section/28/enacted (accessed 10 June 2019).

Hall, F (2016) *Getting Started: A Toolkit for Preventing and Tackling Homophobic, Biphobic and Transphobic Bullying in Schools*. London: Stonewall.

Ofsted (2013) *Exploring the School's Actions to Prevent and Tackle Homophobic and Transphobic Bullying*. London: Ofsted.

Ofsted (2017) *School Inspection Handbook*. Manchester: Ofsted.

Stonewall (2015) *Teachers' Report*. London: Stonewall.

Thomas, G (2014) *Proud: My Autobiography*. London: Ebury Press.

8. DISADVANTAGED CHILDREN

Key issues

Issues around the attainment and experiences of children deemed disadvantaged has been a prominent feature of the educational landscape for a number of years, and, while changing in nature to some extent, this thorny deep-rooted issue very much remains. Ofsted, in its 2016 report *Unknown Children: Destined for Disadvantage?* notes that '*Disadvantage is a complex issue. It can affect children from birth and, left unchecked and unchallenged, can impact negatively on every aspect of a child's life*' (p 11). The issue of disadvantage is vast, but this chapter will explore how it can be tackled in a primary school context with a particular focus on effective use of the Pupil Premium Grant (PPG).

The Pupil Premium Grant

In an attempt to address the attainment gap between pupils from disadvantaged backgrounds and their peers, the government introduced the PPG in 2011. This is additional funding, targeted at eligible pupils, to address the attainment gap between disadvantaged children and their non-disadvantaged peers. While there continues to be speculation about the future of the PPG, it remains as a driver for improvement. It is pertinent to note that disadvantage is not just about economic poverty but could relate to family, social or environmental circumstances. Children of all abilities are eligible for PPG, and it is vital to remember that disadvantage does not equate to low ability; indeed, issues around more able learners must be considered. To qualify for PPG, children are either:

· looked after by the local authority;
· eligible for free school meals (FSM) at any point within the last six years (known as Ever 6 children);
· from a family in which their parent(s) are currently serving in the armed forces.

The introduction of Universal Credit has seen some reduction in eligible numbers for PPG, and Universal Infant Free School Meals has meant that some children who may be eligible for the funding do not qualify as their parents and carers do not realise that they need to apply for FSM in order to be eligible. Unsurprisingly, with budget restraints, many schools have been proactive in ensuring that parents and carers do apply.

ACCOUNTABILITY

Naturally, with the high level of investment of public money, the government and Ofsted are very much focused on the impact of PPG in 'closing the gap' or 'diminishing differences' between disadvantaged children and their non-disadvantaged peers. The impact, in this sense, is still not evident, and the future of PPG hangs in the balance. The EEF Annual Report (January 2018) noted, *'There will be little or no headway in closing the gap between disadvantaged pupils and their classmates in the next 5 years – but there is still an opportunity for secondary schools to make a difference.'*

SCHOOL STRATEGY AND WEBSITE COMPLIANCE

It is paramount that all schools have a clear strategy in relation to PPG to ensure that funding is spent in a strategic manner; focused on outcomes. This information must be published on the school's website in an accessible manner. DfE guidance clearly states that this must include:

· how much money the school has received for Pupil Premium;
· identification of the main barriers to educational achievement;

- how the money will be spent in order to address these barriers, with clear and measurable objectives;
- a rationale for the spending strategy;
- an explanation of how impact on attainment and progress will be measured.

This strategy must be reviewed every academic year, but more regular monitoring is essential to ensure impact. Information from the previous academic year must also be reported on the school's website in terms of how PPG was spent and the impact it had. It is essential that DfE guidance on school website compliance is checked regularly and audited by relevant school staff and governors.

Early intervention

Early intervention has been a key theme in much of the policy related to education in the past decade as the importance of the formative years is emphasised. In 2016, Ofsted noted that, '*a gap in children's speech and language equivalent to 19 months has already emerged for some children in the lowest income families before they have even started statutory school*' (p 14). This shows the importance of early action so that such gaps can be addressed through targeted intervention. Multi-agency working is also a key to success because schools need to understand the broader issues affecting families that may result in potential barriers to learning for children to ensure that no time is lost in putting into place the most appropriate support.

BUDGET CUTS

Discussion about budget cuts and their impact on schools is rarely out of the news, and these are impacting upon PPG usage. The Sutton Trust Annual Survey of teachers (2017) reports that 30 per cent of the head teachers surveyed had used PPG funding to plug gaps in school budgets. This is at odds with considering how the money could be best spent on those children it is meant for so as to positively impact upon their educational achievement, attainment and progress as well as their life chances. Ofsted has a clear agenda to ensure that the PPG benefits those for whom it is intended. Many schools have seen a reduction in support staff, with TES (2018) reporting that 80 per cent of heads reduced the number or hours of support staff in 2017–18, demonstrating an increase on the previous academic year. This has meant the need for low-cost, high-impact strategies, such as growth mindset, which is explored in Chapter 9. This readiness to learn is the most basic need for effective learning in school and is something that you need to reflect upon in relation to your pupils.

Evidence-informed approaches

The importance of evidence-informed practice in schools is widely acknowledged and is promoted by key figures, including Sir John Dunford (2014). As every child is unique, there is no right or wrong way, necessarily, to cater for your disadvantaged learners. There is no doubt that having definite and clear guidance on how to spend their additional funding would make life easier, but the varied nature of the phenomena makes this impossible. Confidence and staff buy-in to the value of Pupil Premium is needed to ensure careful analysis of each child's specific needs and barriers with a focus on impactful intervention. Dr Lee Elliot Major (2012), chair of the evaluation advisory group of the EEF, famously used the Bananarama principle: 'It ain't what you spend, it's the way that you spend it.' The EEF produced a live online document called *The Teaching and Learning Toolkit* based on international research evidence that identifies a wide range of potential interventions or opportunities and experiences. These are considered in relation to cost, evidence-based credibility and potential impact in terms of months' progress. It is important to note that these have a social and emotional focus as well as an academic one. While not guaranteed to impact on your children, this gives a good starting point.

The Sutton Trust is another prime source of evidence-based research to inform your practice. It works with children and their families from birth throughout their education to ensure access and opportunity to the best life chances by overcoming a range of barriers. It is essential that your school's Pupil Premium leader is proactive in engaging with such sources and disseminating key findings that will impact upon provision and drive best practice. All teachers have a professional duty to remain up to date with the latest developments and use guidance reports such as the EEF reports about 'Making Best Use of Teaching Assistants' and 'Improving Literacy for Primary-Aged Pupils at Key Stages 1 and 2' to ensure that your approaches are guided by best practice and credible academic research.

Good practice example

CONSIDERING HOW ADAPTATIONS TO SCHOOL POLICY CAN ENHANCE CHILDREN'S ABILITY AND READINESS TO LEARN

Start with a comprehensive review of the school's behaviour policy to ensure a consistent and unerring focus on the positives with rewards that have immediacy (for example, a golden ticket). While the policy is important, you need to ensure whole-staff buy-in and training. The focus here is on preparing the children to learn. In the mornings, the child(ren) in need of support should be met by an adult and have time to talk with that adult, following a format such as HOPE (Helping Our Pupils' Emotions) (www.burdenbasket.co.uk). The behaviour policy should be simple in format; five key rules, which are consistently understood and implemented by all stakeholders, is a good number. The focus should be positive throughout; for example, instead of 'Stop running along the corridor', say, 'I like the way you are about to walk along the corridor.' You will also need to work with parents in order to break down any barriers that may exist. (These may not be a result of your work but their own experiences in education.) Regularly communicate with parents and make time for face-to-face meetings, for example on the path at the beginning or end of the school day. Instead of using report cards, use positive behaviour logs. The resourcing for such activities (for Pupil Premium children) could come from the PPG, and evidence in relation to their behaviour and resulting attainment in class can be used to show the impact of such initiatives.

Good practice example

THE PERSISTENTLY LATE CHILD

Children who are persistently absent or late will be missing important learning time. Here, the PPG could be used to buy alarm clocks for the children or parents or fund the child's attendance at a school breakfast club so that the child is in school earlier and has breakfast before the school day commences. An adult could be available (funding could be used here too) to talk to the children using HOPE strategies to help them get ready for the school day. If the timetable is fairly constant, for example with a phonics session at the start of the school day, the child's punctuality and engagement in school will mean that, at a basic level, they can access the learning as a result of being present. This can have a significant impact on the attainment of some disadvantaged children.

Quality-first teaching

Quality-first teaching is a phrase frequently heard in discussions around disadvantaged children. It refers to teaching that is focused, based on clear objectives and that engages pupils through dialogue in a range of contexts. Teachers act as facilitators through the use of modelling and questioning. Children are expected to take ownership of their learning in a positive and rewarding environment. Aspiration shines through this approach. To be effective, CPD (continuing professional development) in schools should focus on teaching rather than just intervention – particularly important when considering budgetary restraints. For it to be truly impactful, there needs to be buy-in and commitment from the whole staff with everyone understanding the range of barriers through the use of provision maps. Sir John Dunford (2014) reinforces the need to have an '*unerring focus on the quality of teaching.*' While the importance of high-quality teaching is manifest, this is not going to have an impact if attendance and punctuality are issues. These also need to be swiftly acted upon if outcomes are to be enhanced.

Awareness of emerging trends

The drive for quality-first teaching is now well established and is showing an impact on outcomes for pupils. Having said this, you need to stay up to date with the latest trends and issues as they need to be addressed and will form the focus for inspection. A key vulnerable group, currently, is white British (disadvantaged) boys. Knowing the nature of vulnerable groups in relation to your school population is essential. Here, the issues around aspiration are notable, reflected in Damian Hinds emphasising the need to increase the numbers of these boys going to university. Issues around low aspirations may well stem from parents, and the issue is much broader than the school. To this end, you need to consider the opportunities and experiences children have had and how you may open up possibilities that have not been encountered or considered before. Enrichment activities are worthy of note here as these are the key to enhancing outcomes. These may take a range of forms, including educational visits, extracurricular clubs and forest school, amongst many others. You need to have a clear understanding of vulnerable groups and carefully consider what may be done to achieve change and implement this in an appropriate manner. It is important to note that implementation of any initiative is a process and not a one-off or short-term event. It needs to be carefully structured and planned based on well-founded research and then regularly evaluated in terms of its impact on specific groups. When planning any intervention, you need to have a clear understanding of the particular barriers to learning that these groups are facing so as to be able to plan strategically to address them.

Effective deployment of teaching assistants

Reduced numbers of teaching assistants mean that, more than ever before, you need to consider how you are deploying teaching assistants effectively so as to maximise their impact on outcomes for children. There are clear benefits to this, including managing your workload as a teacher more effectively as well as the rich benefits they can bring to pupil learning. It is important that schools carefully consider and strategically plan for the continuing professional development of teaching assistants to enable them to impact on outcomes for children through the provision of timely and focused intervention based on a depth of subject and pedagogical knowledge. This can involve challenging previously held views about teaching assistant deployment. The EEF 'Making Best Use of Teaching Assistants' guidance report (2016) and other research-informed sources should be used to focus your reflection on how effectively you deploy your teaching assistants in relation to pupil learning and outcomes. This remains high on the national agenda as it has been branded a high-cost low-impact approach to supporting disadvantaged children, contradicting what is seen as best practice through low-cost high-impact strategies. Not only do you need to plan for quality deployment, you need to regularly review the effectiveness of the approaches used with specific children.

In the spotlight

Data is essential when considering and evidencing impact of any kind. To keep Pupil Premium children high on the agenda, it is important that pupil progress and performance-management meetings, in addition to everything else, have a definite focus on this specific group of learners. Regular monitoring and reviews of data are essential to ensure best outcomes. It is also important that you set higher targets to demonstrate aspiration for disadvantaged children and to reflect the additional resource that will be available to support them in making good progress. Data can be tricky, and knowing the individual needs of all children is important when deciding which data best tells their story. Soft data, such as that gleaned from initiatives including Positive Play, Boxall Profiles and Strength and Difficulty Questionnaires (SDQs) can show the impact of initiatives undertaken in a way that more traditional data may not. To show progress and have a true understanding of the impact, entry and exit data should be used to provide a narrative for individual children. Their academic data may tell one story, but the needs are so complex that a broader range is needed related to the extent to which specific barriers have been overcome. The centrality of effective governance through a Pupil Premium link governor is paramount as this ensures accountability through challenging dialogue with a focus on outcomes and driving best practice. Primary schools have made significant headway in terms of their provision for disadvantaged children which is increasingly tailored to very specific and complex needs, but the concern remains around continuity and sustainability when children move to secondary. The data collected during primary is a key part of this puzzle, but dialogue needs to continue between relevant parties to ensure continuity and the best provision throughout transition periods.

The small numbers of disadvantaged children within a school can result in misleading or relatively meaningless data, so case studies are an important part of the storytelling behind the raw figures. Case studies can also help to identify the rate of progress, and if this slows the need to instigate intervention swiftly. A case study should include the following information:

- personal details about the pupil;
- information about the outcomes for the pupil prior to the intervention to support;
- details about the intervention or support, including timing allocation and resources deployed;
- assessment of outcomes, including consideration of how this differs from children who are not eligible for the PPG (to show impact on the in-school gap) and how this differs from the national average for all pupils (to show impact on the school-versus-national gap).

Pupil Premium Plus

Pupil Premium Plus is additional funding that was introduced in 2013 for children who are either looked after or have previously been looked after. This includes children who are fostered, adopted or under special guardianship (when living with family, for example grandparents). Fostered children are entitled to Personalised Education Plan meetings with a social worker, and it is important to understand the support that fostered children are entitled to as opposed to those who are adopted or under special guardianship. Having said that, it is considered good practice to have meetings with special guardianship parents and carers too as this reinforces the notion of aspirations for all. While you need to fulfil statutory duties, it is also essential that you consider what is best practice, based on research and guidance, to impact on the outcomes for all children.

Summary

The key themes related to successful provision for disadvantaged children centre around knowing and responding to the various needs of all these children through creative strategies which are clearly measured by means of a range of data. The quality of teaching is central to everything, and monitoring of impact must inform you of when adaptations are needed. Engagement of all parties with a focus on aspiration is vital, and these positive messages need constant reinforcement.

Policy summary

POLICY	KEY POINTS	IMPLICATIONS FOR SCHOOLS
PUPIL PREMIUM: FUNDING AND ACCOUNTABILITY FOR SCHOOLS (DFE/ EDUCATION AND SKILLS FUNDING AGENCY)	· THIS KEY DOCUMENT OUTLINES THE AMOUNT OF FUNDING THAT SCHOOLS WILL RECEIVE. INFORMATION IS PROVIDED IN TERMS OF HOW THE FUNDING SHOULD BE SPENT AND HOW THE GOVERNMENT WILL HOLD SCHOOLS TO ACCOUNT.	· UNDERSTAND THE AMOUNT OF FUNDING RECEIVED PER ELIGIBLE PUPIL. · ENGAGE WITH RESEARCH-INFORMED APPROACHES, PARTICULARLY THAT PRODUCED BY THE EEF. · USE THE FAMILIES OF SCHOOLS DATABASE TO ENGAGE WITH GOOD PRACTICE IN SIMILAR SCHOOLS. · USE THE EEF DIY EVALUATION TOOL TO SUPPORT YOU IN EVALUATING THE IMPACT. · ENGAGE WITH RECOGNISED GOOD PRACTICE (PUPIL PREMIUM AWARDS). · CONSIDER IMPLICATIONS RELATED TO THE REQUIREMENTS OF THE CURRENT OFSTED INSPECTION FRAMEWORK.

POLICY	KEY POINTS	IMPLICATIONS FOR SCHOOLS
		· ENSURE COMPLIANCE WITH ONLINE REPORTING.
PUPIL PREMIUM: ALLOCATIONS AND CONDITIONS OF GRANT (EDUCATION AND SKILLS FUNDING AGENCY)	· DETAILS HOW THE PPG SHOULD BE SPENT.	· UNDERSTAND KEY INFORMATION, INCLUDING PUPIL ELIGIBILITY AND HOW THE PPG SHOULD BE SPENT. · ENGAGE WITH THE DOCUMENT FOR THE CURRENT ACADEMIC YEAR.
OFSTED SCHOOL INSPECTION HANDBOOK (SEPTEMBER 2018)	· SETS OUT THE CURRENT INSPECTION FRAMEWORK FOR SCHOOLS.	· NOTE PARAGRAPHS 192-4 (pp 59-60) AND GRADE DESCRIPTORS ON pp 62-3. · FOCUS ON PUPILS' PROGRESS FROM STARTING POINTS. · ENSURE DATA PROVIDED IS MEANINGFUL, PARTICULARLY IN THE CONTEXT OF SMALL GROUPS. · BE CLEAR ABOUT THE IMPACT OF CURRENT PROVISION IN TERMS OF 'REDUCING DIFFERENCES.' · CONSIDER ISSUES AROUND THE QUALITY OF TEACHING, BEHAVIOUR AND CURRICULUM PROVISION. · BE CLEAR ABOUT ANY SHORTFALL IN PROGRESS OR ATTAINMENT FOR DISADVANTAGED CHILDREN AND IDENTIFY WHAT IS BEING DONE TO ADDRESS THIS.
THE SERVICE PUPIL PREMIUM - WHAT YOU NEED TO KNOW (MINISTRY OF DEFENCE)	· EMPHASISES THE DISTINCTION BETWEEN SERVICE PUPIL PREMIUM AND PUPIL PREMIUM.	· NOTE THE DISTINCTION BETWEEN PUPIL PREMIUM AND SERVICE PUPIL PREMIUM. · CONSIDER HOW SERVICE PUPIL PREMIUM IS BEING USED TO PROVIDE PASTORAL SUPPORT, PARTICULARLY DURING CHALLENGING TIMES.

POLICY	KEY POINTS	IMPLICATIONS FOR SCHOOLS
		• CONSIDER EXPERIENCES THAT WILL HELP CHILDREN TO UNDERSTAND THE ROLE THEIR PARENT PLAYS IN THE SERVICE AND TO SUPPORT THEM IN COPING WITH THE POTENTIAL STRAINS OF MILITARY LIFE. • ENSURE SEPARATE ACCOUNTING FOR PUPIL PREMIUM AND SERVICE PUPIL PREMIUM – EVIDENCE OF THE DISTINCTION WILL BE REQUIRED BY OFSTED.

❖ Critical questions

1. Do you know and understand the barriers faced by children deemed disadvantaged in your class?

2. What do you and your school do to engage with the parents of disadvantaged children? What impact has this had on outcomes for those children?

3. How do you record assessment information and what does this say about the differences between disadvantaged children and their non-disadvantaged counterparts? What might the potential reasons be for this emerging picture?

4. What is your school's strategy for PPG spending? What does this tell you about the impact of your spending on outcomes for children?

5. Is information related to PPG easily accessible on your school website?

6. Is the information on your website compliant with current DfE regulations? How is this verified, for example is it scrutinised by a governor?

7. Is your PPG strategy reviewed annually? Aside from the annual monitoring, how often is your PPG strategy monitored, and how effective is this?

8. What do you do to ensure early intervention so that children have full opportunity to be successful?

9. How efficient are the strategies you deploy in terms of cost versus impact?

10. Which research has informed your approach and why? What has the impact been in your school?

11. Which are the key vulnerable groups in your setting and what are you doing to address this? Why have you adopted this approach?

12. How well embedded is quality-first teaching in your school? How do you know? What could be done to further enhance this?

13. How effectively are teaching assistants deployed? How do you know? How has research informed your (school's) approach to teaching-assistant deployment?

14. What could be done to further enhance the effectiveness of teaching-assistant deployment in your school?

15. How effectively are you reviewing the impact of various interventions?

16. What could be done to enhance the effectiveness of these?

17. How do you ensure that your disadvantaged children remain high on the agenda? Is there anything that could enhance the visibility of these children?

18. What type of data do you collect to show impact? Is this effective and is there potential to draw upon a broader range?

19. How effectively does the school's link governor support and challenge practice related to disadvantaged children?

20. How do you ensure the best outcomes for Pupil Premium Plus children?

21. How creatively have you used the PPG to address the specific needs of disadvantaged children to ensure their access to learning in order to support progress and attainment?

22. Are you aware of potential interventions, such as various types of therapy which may be free? In cases like these, could you use the PPG to pay for transport?

23. Do disadvantaged children have access to the full range of after-school clubs? Is finance causing a barrier to participation? How might this be impacting on their range of experiences and what might the impact be in terms of their aspirations?

24. Do you ensure separation between PPG and SPP? What evidence do you use to show impact and how effectively does this show the distinction?

further reading and resources

EEF Teaching and Learning Toolkit (https://educationendowmentfoundation. org.uk/evidence-summaries/ teaching-learning-toolkit)	This is an online/live resource which provides access to a range of international evidence related to the teaching of 5–16 year-olds. This should be used as a guide when considering the most appropriate interventions.
Making Best Use of Teaching Assistants (https://educationendowmentfoundation. org.uk/tools/guidance-reports/ making-best-use-of-teaching-assistants)	A research-informed guide to maximising the effectiveness of teaching assistants.
The Sutton Trust (www.suttontrust.com)	An organisation that specialises in evidence-based research with a view to enhancing social mobility.
John Dunford Consulting (https:// johndunfordconsulting.co.uk)	The website of the former national Pupil Premium Champion. Some very useful articles about the Pupil Premium.
Pupil Premium Awards (www. pupilpremiumawards.co.uk/ppawards2017/ en/page/home)	A showcase of some very effective practice regarding provision for disadvantaged children with case studies that share successful approaches.
Head Teacher Update (www.headteacher- update.com/best-practice/pupil-premium/ 693128)	Not just for heads! This is an accessible website that shares some best-practice approaches related to the Pupil Premium.
DfE (November 2015), Supporting the Attainment of Disadvantaged Pupils: Briefing for School Leaders (https://assets. publishing.service.gov.uk/government/ uploads/system/uploads/attachment_data/ file/473976/DFE-RS411_Supporting_the_ attainment_of_disadvantaged_pupils_-_ briefing_for_school_leaders.pdf)	An evidence-informed document that provides a useful background to the Pupil Premium and notes key features of success and good practice.
EEF Families of Schools Database (https:// educationendowmentfoundation.org.uk/ tools/families-of-schools-database)	This enables schools to find schools with a similar context in order to engage with good practice and learn from this.
EEF DIY Evaluation Tool (https:// educationendowmentfoundation.org.uk/ tools/diy-guide/getting-started)	This is a tool to support schools in evaluating the impact of approaches taken.

References

Department for Education (2018) Pupil Premium: Funding and Accountability for Schools. [online] Available at: www.gov.uk/guidance/pupil-premium-information-for-schools-and-alternative-provision-settings (accessed 10 April 2019).

Dunford, J (2014) Ten-Point Plan for Spending the Pupil Premium Successfully. [online] Available at: https://johndunfordconsulting.co.uk/2014/10/11/ten-point-plan-for-spending-the-pupil-premium-successfully/ (accessed 10 April 2019).

Education Endowment Foundation (2016) Making Best Use of Teaching Assistants. [online] Available at: https://educationendowmentfoundation.org.uk/tools/guidance-reports/making-best-use-of-teaching-assistants (accessed 10 April 2019).

Education Endowment Foundation (2018) Annual Report, 2017. [online] Available at: https://educationendowmentfoundation.org.uk/public/files/Annual_Reports/EEF_Annual_Report_2016-17_-_interactive.pdf (accessed 10 April 2019).

Elliot Major, L (2012) Follow the Banarama Principle: With the pupil premium, it ain't what you do, it's the way that you do it, says Lee Elliot Major. [online] Available at: www.tes.com/news/follow-bananarama-principle (accessed 15 April 2019).

Ofsted (2016) *Unknown Children: Destined for Disadvantage?* London: Ofsted.

Sutton Trust (2017) Teacher Polling 2017. [online] Available at: www.suttontrust.com/research-paper/pupil-premium-polling-2017-teachers-school-budget/ (accessed 10 April 2019).

TES (2018) Rise in Schools Cutting Teachers and Support Staff to Balance Books. [online] Available at: www.tes.com/news/rise-schools-cutting-teachers-and-support-staff-balance-books (accessed 10 April 2019).

9. MENTAL HEALTH AND WELL-BEING FOR CHILDREN

The mental health and well-being of children and young people is a significant and growing cause for concern in society. The Childline annual review (NSPCC, 2018) highlighted that mental and emotional health were in the top three concerns reported in 2017/18. In 2018, the National Health Service (NHS) reported that one in eight children and young people between the ages of 5 and 19 have a mental health disorder. While no definite cause was attributed to this significant figure, it may be considered to result from austerity, academic pressures and social media. The Mental Health Green Paper (Department of Health and the DfE, 2017) has further reinforced the importance of mental health visibility and proactively dealing with this issue. The House of Commons Committee of Public Accounts (2019) notes the importance of mental health services for children and young people developing ways to support children's mental health through prevention and early intervention. There are growing calls for mental health support to be embedded within schools in order to meet the needs of children. From September 2019, the new Ofsted category 'Personal Development' will consider how effectively schools look after the mental health of children. This chapter unpicks a range of issues that you need to consider in relation to children's mental health and explores strategies that can be implemented to address the issues.

It is important that you bear these points in mind throughout the course of your work with children and their families as it has been noted that emotional well-being can be overlooked, ignored or explained only in terms of behaviour. Being alert to the potential mental and emotional well-being issues that may be at play is key to having a positive impact on outcomes for children and their families. Matt Hancock, Health Secretary, said, '*I want to see all children and young people have the opportunity to flourish – and protecting their mental health is vital to this*' (GOV.UK, 2019).

What is mental health?

Dr Mike Condra (2013) provides a helpful definition of mental health and talks about how this is not wall-to-wall happiness. We will all experience a full range of emotions. He notes three aspects of mental wellness:

1. engagement in productive activities that engage the senses and intellect;
2. fulfilling relationships which are based on reciprocity;
3. adaptability which enables us to be flexible to change, cope with adversity and identify other possibilities when problems arise.

In contrast, he notes the features of mental distress:

1. difficulty concentrating and memory issues;
2. mood: anxious, sad, irritable with a loss of a sense of pleasure;
3. behaviour issues, including eating and sleeping.

In addition, the World Health Organization (2014) notes that mental health is '*a state of well-being in which every individual realises his or her own potential, can cope with the normal stresses of life, can work productively and fruitfully, and is able to make a contribution to his or her own community.*'

These definitions are helpful in enabling you to be alert to where there may be potential mental-health issues that need to be addressed. In addition to your alertness, children also need to be made aware of these points through your curriculum. If you notice personality changes, agitation, withdrawal, poor self-care and a sense of hopelessness, you need to take action.

Mental health and behaviour

In November 2018, the DfE published non-statutory guidance on mental health and behaviour in an attempt to support children whose behaviour stems from mental health problems. The guidance identifies key points and principles, including the central role played by schools in enabling children to be resilient in order to support and promote good mental health and well-being. The document notes the importance of a consistent whole-school approach to mental health and well-being. While you have a role to play in supporting identification, it is noted that only those appropriately qualified should be allowed to diagnose. It states that teachers should, '*observe children day-to-day and identify those whose behaviour suggests that they may be experiencing a mental health problem or be at risk of developing one. This may include withdrawn pupils whose needs may otherwise go unrecognised*' (DfE, 2018, p 12).

Good practice example

EMOTION COACHING

Please see the article about this approach at https://schoolsimprovement.net/emotion-coaching-brings-best-children. This is an approach to behaviour management that develops social and emotional skills rather than using rewards and sanctions so as to provide greater ownership for the child.

It is based on two key elements:

1. empathy: recognising and labelling emotions, regardless of behaviour so as to promote self-awareness;
2. guidance: helping a child to recognise and label emotions and feelings.

Children's worlds

You need to acknowledge the range of experiences that surround any individual child, including their knowledge and understanding of a range of issues, including:

- mental health;
- relationships;
- school ethos;
- academic pressures;
- social media;

- world events;
- money worries;
- bullying;
- loneliness;
- identity.

With these in mind, you will be more alert to how one or a combination of these may impact on a child's mental health and well-being. The Mental Health Foundation (2019) notes that approximately 10 per cent of children are affected by mental health problems which often arise from their surroundings. They highlight that 70 per cent of these children have not had *'appropriate interventions at a sufficiently early age'* (Mental Health Foundation, 2019a). Mental health and well-being are coming to the fore as part of the revised Ofsted inspection framework with part of this being a consideration of how school leadership enables pupils to overcome barriers to learning. To address this, you need to have an astute understanding of what these barriers are for each individual.

FAMILY DEBT

The Children's Society (2016) produced a research paper entitled *The Damage of Debt*. This noted that children from low-income households are more likely to have poor mental health and that children in families with multiple debt issues are at a greater risk of experiencing mental health problems. Experiences of debt led to both parents and children feeling stressed, anxious and depressed as well as ashamed and embarrassed. It notes how children feel guilty about not being able to help with debt and that arguments arise between family members because of the debt. While teachers have limited options to support with this, it is important to note the impact that living in poverty or with significant debt can have on children's mental health and well-being as well as their physical and material needs. This may impact on how Pupil Premium money is utilised.

PARENTAL MENTAL ILL HEALTH AND CHILD CARERS

The Mental Health Foundation (2019b) estimates there to be around 175,000 children in the UK who are carers for either a parent or a family member with mental health problems. With this responsibility, there are a number of factors that have the potential to negatively impact on a variety of elements of children's well-being, including their mental health, and support for them is variable. Education around, and visibility of, mental health in the curriculum is important, first in contributing to children's understanding of the issues they are dealing with and second in recognition of potential support strategies that may be relevant to the case of their parent. This emphasises the importance of making mental health visible throughout the curriculum to ensure children do not feel isolated and to break any stigma that may exist.

ACADEMIC PRESSURES

Headlines are constantly published related to the academic pressures on children. The Oxford Open Learning Trust (FE News, 2019) has highlighted that 33 per cent of primary-school parents note the stress caused to their children by exams with 40 per cent of parents with 5–11 year-olds considering that too much pressure is being placed on their children to do well in the tests. These figures are reinforced by the TES (2018), reporting on a YouGov survey that found that 63 per cent of parents feel that their children are under too much pressure which leads to high levels of anxiety and a lack of enjoyment for learning. The Oxford Open Learning Trust research also flagged up issues around homework in that parents believe too much is being set with 13 per cent of primary pupils being expected to spend five hours or more on homework each week.

- It is important that, as a teacher, you consider how children are prepared for tests in an appropriate way, which recognises their importance but places the least amount of stress on children.
- With homework, consider the quality rather than quantity in terms of how effectively it engages the children (and their families) in consolidating their understanding of concepts and supports their progress.
- Regular engagement with children and their parents and carers to find out what is working and where there are issues is an important feature to build into your practice to realise the best outcomes for children both academically but also personally, ensuring the best outcomes in terms of mental health and well-being.

SOCIAL MEDIA

The impact of social media and the online world on children, particularly in terms of mental health, is constantly being drawn to our attention. As with any issue like this there will be a mixture of advantages and disadvantages. It is important to note the idea of balance as no engagement with the experiences offered through social media will have a limiting effect, whereas too much exposure can cause significant problems. Glazzard and Mitchell (2018, p 32) cite data from the Office for National Statistics which highlights that, '*27 per cent of young people who engage with social networking sites for three or more hours per day experience symptoms of mental health compared to 12 per cent of children who spend no time on social networking sites.*'

The issues at play are discussed in greater detail in Chapter 3, but it is important to consider how over-engagement with social media can cause mental health issues surrounding body image, self-image, sleep, anxiety and depression.

WORLD NEWS AND EVENTS

Scary events that happen in the world will inevitably be seen by children through the news, and the Mental Health Foundation (2018) notes how '*it is no longer possible to control the news that we are exposed to or shield children from upsetting information.'* With this in mind, as noted in Chapter 4, it is important that you talk to children in appropriate and balanced ways that enable them to ask questions and make sense of some of the issues as far as possible. Consistency between teachers and parents is paramount in ensuring the best outcomes.

The school curriculum

The curriculum is a key part of your work regarding children's mental health and well-being. Within this, questions about what should and should not be included are critical but incredibly complex. It is important that any curriculum is broad, balanced and inclusive, enabling the full range of children to participate and achieve success and a sense of achievement. Glazzard and Bligh (2018) make a case for engaging children with issues around what mental health is, that it is a spectrum and that mental health can go up and down dependent on life events and experiences as well as the impact that an individual may have on the mental health of others. Armiger (2019) notes a common confusion between mental health and mental ill health. He cites a scale to reinforce the concept of mental health: wellness – stress – distress – illness. Children will have some knowledge and experience of mental health, so it is important that you provide safe, meaningful opportunities to discuss the issues in an informed and balanced manner. You may feel unease about engaging children with issues around mental ill health, but Glazzard and Bligh (2018, p 10) emphasise, '*It is important to normalise and de-stigmatise mental health so that children do not grow up believing that mental health is something that should not be discussed.'* Emphasising that this is by no means an exhaustive list, the key themes that Glazzard and Bligh (2018) suggest for inclusion in a school's mental health curriculum are:

- feelings;
- stress;
- coping with loss;
- social confidence; and
- friendships.

They emphasise that this is by no means an exhaustive list. The importance of weaving mental-health issues throughout the full range of curriculum areas needs to be emphasised so that it is not seen as a distinct issue; it impacts on all aspects of everyone's life. Glazzard and Bostwick (2018, p 82) talk about developing children's emotional literacy and note that an effective curriculum, '*should educate young people about how to recognise and manage their feelings, how to cope with conflict and how to support others who might be in need.'* Bearing in mind the Childline data mentioned at the start of this chapter, it is clear to see why this is such a pressing issue for you as a teacher.

Eight principles to promote emotional health and well-being in education

Public Health England (2015, p 6) identifies eight principles to support effective education in terms of emotional health and well-being. These are:

1. curriculum teaching and learning to promote resilience and support social and emotional learning;
2. enabling student voice to influence decisions;
3. staff development to support their own well-being and that of students;
4. identifying need and monitoring impact of interventions;
5. working with parents/carers;
6. targeted support and appropriate referral;
7. an ethos and environment that promotes respect and values diversity;
8. leadership and management that supports and champions efforts to promote emotional health and well-being. (It is pertinent to note that this is at the centre of the circle which contains all of these elements.)

This is a tool which your school should use in its review and planning for a curriculum that supports the mental health and well-being of children. A key message coming through current documentation is that the promotion of mental health and well-being needs to be embedded within all school policies and procedures to ensure a whole-school approach that actively involves all stakeholders, including children.

Visibility in school

Each year, Children's Mental Health Week is marked in February, and it is a good opportunity to consider how to meaningfully engage children and their parents and carers with issues surrounding mental health during this time. As with all such events, there is a wealth of online resource to support you with the current theme. In February 2019, the government launched one of the largest trials worldwide with the aim of building the evidence base to show what works to support mental health and well-being. It has been noted by Damian Hinds that the main reason for these trials is to enhance the understanding teachers have in order to support children with a range of issues. The trial included:

- mindfulness techniques;
- relaxation strategies;
- breathing exercises to support emotional regulation;
- sessions with experts in the field; and
- mental health assessments.

YOGA

Many schools are including yoga as part of their school week. It is seen to be accessible in terms of children's abilities and cost. Yoga is a technique to engage people's minds, bodies and spirits to promote a sense of well-being. It can support the management of stress through breathing. You should ensure that you encourage and enable children to apply these techniques in relevant contexts; it should not just be something they do in isolation and then forget about when they need it! Bodily awareness is also important in the management of stress. In many ways, yoga is a mindfulness technique as it is about concentration and focus on the present, free from distractions and using this to increase individuals' confidence and sense of well-being in the moment. Remember to make this a regular part of children's experience so that it becomes a natural and routine technique for them to use in order to establish good habits for life, including at home.

What is happiness?

Happiness is difficult to define as it is such an individual and personalised phenomenon. The external signals, ie, people's facial expressions, do not always give us an accurate indication of their happiness. You need to bear in mind that a quiet, introverted child may actually be very happy. As I seem to say so often in this book, it is essential that you know your children as individuals – what is it that really makes them tick? This knowledge will also mean that you can recognise and act upon any changes in behaviour. Some children may have a diagnosis relating to their mental health, and it is often these children who receive a greater focus. While you need to be aware of these children and take appropriate action, you also need to be alert to those without a diagnosis so that timely intervention can be made if necessary.

The importance of talk

At a conference a few years ago, one comment made me really sit up and take note. The speaker noted how teachers understand the need to talk about 'obvious' dangers that children encounter, such as crossing the road, drugs, alcohol and generally keeping safe online and offline, but there is very little talk about mental health. Mental health is actually one of the biggest killers in young people, so talk and access to this supported talk across the curriculum is essential.

EMPATHY

It is easy to confuse the notions of empathy and sympathy. Brown (2013) talks about empathy as a fuel for connection and sympathy as a driver of disconnection. She notes that we will often try to make things better for people, but that this is not always possible. Having said this, by connecting and saying something along the lines of, 'I don't really know what to say, but I am so glad you have told me,' can mean that someone who is at a low point recognises someone is there for them but is not judging them or trying to liken something that has happened to them to the particular situation. Brown (2013) notes the four qualities of empathy, and these can be applied to your role as a teacher in your interactions as well as the guidance you provide your children about engaging with others:

1. perspective-taking;

2. staying out of judgement;

3. recognising emotions in other people;

4. communicating that emotion.

ACTIVE LISTENING

When listening to someone, it is very easy to be distracted in numerous ways, but it is important that you and the children recognise the importance of being in the moment and really focusing on what is happening. Taking account of the following points will be of benefit.

- What are they saying explicitly?
- What are they not saying?
- Where is the emotion?
- What do they repeatedly say?

EMOTIONAL INTELLIGENCE

Earlier in this chapter, the importance of engaging children with the concept of mental health was noted. Linked with this is the development of emotional intelligence, which relates to the ability to recognise and manage one's own feelings and will influence how one deals with problems when they occur. In addition to the personal side of emotional intelligence, it will also enable an individual to recognise and understand the feelings of others. The development of emotional intelligence will also support the development of children's resilience as it will give them a voice by enabling them to unpick various elements, including:

- thoughts (eg, nobody in this classroom likes me);
- feelings (eg, I feel anxious);
- actions (eg, I will disrupt the lesson so that I get sent out and then I will not feel anxious).

An emotionally intelligent child will be:

- confident;
- resilient;
- optimistic;
- self-aware;
- self-disciplined;
- courageous;
- cooperative;
- communicative;
- long term in their outlook and have goals.

An issue here is when children's needs are not met as this can lead to them having negative thoughts and emotions heavily engrained. As a teacher, you have a key role to play in being alert to concerns and creating an inclusive environment that accommodates children with emotional issues and seeks to educate children in managing and dealing with their problems effectively.

Growth mindset

Many schools are adopting the idea of growth mindset, based on the work of Dr Carol Dweck. This is key to developing a resilience that ensures effective and productive learning behaviours. There is research that suggests that young people with a growth mindset are less likely to demonstrate symptoms of mental illness than those with a fixed mindset. This approach is not a quick fix and will take time to embed as it relies on children developing attitudes to learning that are positive and talking in terms of ongoing development, for example instead of negatively dwelling on making a mistake, recognising that mistakes help us to learn more effectively. Fixed mindset approaches may see children identifying themselves as no good at something, giving up and so on, whereas growth mindset approaches will seek the positive elements and promote perseverance. You will need to consider how you model such attitudes to children as well as the language you use on a daily basis. Having said all of this, the notion of growth mindset does need to be applied with some caution. It could be that children interpret praise for effort as meaning their ability is poor. It is an approach which has been open to misinterpretation with a danger of promoting the idea that anyone can achieve anything they want to. Busch (2018) argues that, *'to help shape students' behaviours and mindsets, teachers should look to develop a consistent culture of high expectations and quality feedback.'* The key point here is that seeing possibilities is more powerful than closing down at the first hurdle in furthering academic achievement as well as developing positive lifelong attitudes.

Good practice example

USE OF STORY

As with any difficult issue, story can be a good way in to exploring or raising awareness of an issue, while depersonalising an issue from an individual to an extent. Two examples of stories that could be used are:

- *The Red Tree* by Shaun Tan
- *Lucy's Blue Day* by Chris Duke

The use of images is particularly powerful so these could be displayed either through the book or a larger image on the interactive whiteboard. There are video versions of some stories as well. As you plan for the session, consider how you will stop, allow time to unpick and enable reflection about the messages being given. It is also important to consider how safe children feel in the environment and to facilitate a space where they may take some time out if they have been affected by a particular issue. The story could, ideally, be part of a larger piece of work that really enables the children to explore and unpick the messages stemming from the narrative. You could use the story as a basis for putting skills around active listening and empathetic talk into practice.

Attachment

Attachment is a significant issue that you need to have at the forefront of your mind. Emotions can be frightening things for children, particularly when they do not know how to deal with them. As a teacher, you need to emphasise that having emotions is normal. Empathy and understanding are key attributes teachers need to have when considering attachment and trauma. The Attachment Research Community (ARC, 2019) notes the huge influence of environment for children. For children who have struggled forming attachments, schools can be a place of safety. The Education Support Partnership (2018) highlights that, '*Students more at risk of developing a mental health problem are those from a care background, adopted or fostered, have learning difficulties or have a chaotic or disadvantaged home life.*'

Emotion coaching in these circumstances can also hold many benefits. The ARC (2019) recognises teachers' concerns about being experts on such issues but states that to make a difference, '*You just need to be able to establish and maintain positive relationships.*' Again, having the awareness is going to have an impact on your work and outcomes for children in all regards.

Mental health first aid

Mental health first aid is an approach that has been adopted in some schools. It is based on the principle of early intervention and support before an individual is then moved on to more specialist and focused support. Even if your school is not adopting the idea wholesale, there is a useful acronym which you could use to support the work you do at the early stages of potential mental-health issues with children.

A   attend, acknowledge, ask;

L   listen actively: let the person tell their story;

E   empathise, explore, evaluate;

R   risk review, retell, refer;

T   take action, track progress, take care (of yourself).

Summary

Mental health and well-being are huge challenges currently facing teachers. This chapter has identified issues to consider as well as some approaches to address these. Modelling and developing respectful relationships that are positive in nature will play a key role in enhancing outcomes for children as they move forward.

Policy summary

POLICY	KEY POINTS	IMPLICATIONS FOR SCHOOLS
OFSTED	• FROM SEPTEMBER 2019, THERE WILL BE A NEW CATEGORY ENTITLED 'PERSONAL DEVELOPMENT.' AT THE TIME OF WRITING, THE FINAL INSPECTION HANDBOOK WAS NOT PUBLISHED, BUT IT SEEMS THAT HOW EFFECTIVELY SCHOOLS LOOK AFTER THE MENTAL HEALTH AND WELL-BEING OF CHILDREN WILL BE SCRUTINISED.	• ENSURE BEST PRACTICE AND FULL COMPLIANCE WITH REQUIREMENTS.

POLICY	KEY POINTS	IMPLICATIONS FOR SCHOOLS
MENTAL HEALTH AND BEHAVIOUR IN SCHOOLS (DFE, 2018)	· THIS NON-STATUTORY ADVICE EMPHASISES THE IMPORTANT ROLE PLAYED BY SCHOOLS IN PROMOTING THE RESILIENCE OF CHILDREN. IT EXPLORES HOW SCHOOLS CAN PROMOTE THE MENTAL HEALTH AND WELL-BEING OF PUPILS.	· CONSIDER HOW YOUR SCHOOL CAN DEMONSTRATE BEST PRACTICE BY FOLLOWING THE GUIDANCE CONTAINED WITHIN. · USE pp 14–15 TO IDENTIFY RISK AND PROTECTIVE FACTORS WHICH ARE BELIEVED TO BE ASSOCIATED WITH MENTAL HEALTH OUTCOMES.
	· THIS CONSIDERS ISSUES AROUND SCHOOL CULTURE WHICH ENABLES PROBLEMS TO BE DISCUSSED IN A SUPPORTIVE AND NON-JUDGEMENTAL WAY, CPD WITH A FOCUS ON EARLY RECOGNITION AND INTERVENTION AS WELL AS CLEAR SYSTEMS AND PROCESSES TO SUPPORT THOSE IN NEED.	
TRANSFORMING CHILDREN AND YOUNG PEOPLE'S MENTAL HEALTH PROVISION: GREEN PAPER (DOH AND DFE, 2017)	· SETS OUT THE FUTURE OF PROVISION AND RESOURCE RELATED TO MENTAL HEALTH.	· NOTE THE IMPLICATIONS OF THIS AS THEY ARISE. THIS MAY BE IN TERMS OF STAFFING, BUT ALSO IN THE IDENTIFICATION OF RESOURCES.
COUNSELLING IN SCHOOLS (DFE, FEBRUARY 2016)	· THIS NON-STATUTORY ADVICE EMPHASISES THE USE OF PSHE TO TEACH ABOUT MENTAL HEALTH. IT ALSO TALKS ABOUT USING ENRICHMENT ACTIVITIES TO FOCUS ON MENTAL HEALTH.	· CONSIDER ASPECTS OF THIS GUIDANCE WHICH ARE SUITABLE TO YOUR PARTICULAR SETTING AND REVIEW HOW EFFECTIVELY YOUR CURRICULUM OFFER INCLUDES COVERAGE OF MENTAL-HEALTH ISSUES.

POLICY	KEY POINTS	IMPLICATIONS FOR SCHOOLS
SUPPORTING PUPILS AT SCHOOL WITH MEDICAL CONDITIONS (DFE, DECEMBER 2015)	· THIS STATUTORY GUIDANCE EMPHASISES THAT IT REFERS TO MENTAL HEALTH AS WELL AS PHYSICAL HEALTH.	· ENSURE THAT THE MENTAL AND EMOTIONAL HEALTH NEEDS OF CHILDREN ARE FULLY ACCOUNTED FOR AND THAT APPROPRIATE EVIDENCE IS KEPT FOR THIS.
PROMOTING CHILDREN AND YOUNG PEOPLE'S EMOTIONAL HEALTH AND WELL-BEING: A WHOLE SCHOOL AND COLLEGE APPROACH (PUBLIC HEALTH ENGLAND, MARCH 2015).	· GUIDANCE FOR SCHOOLS BASED ON EIGHT PRINCIPLES THAT HAVE THE POTENTIAL TO ENHANCE EMOTIONAL HEALTH AND WELL-BEING IN EDUCATIONAL SETTINGS.	· REFLECT ON CURRENT PRACTICE IN RELATION TO THE EIGHT PRINCIPLES. · SHARE AND CELEBRATE BEST PRACTICE. · IDENTIFY A PLAN OF ACTION TO ENHANCE PRACTICE AND ENSURE CONSISTENCY.
SUPPORTING MENTAL HEALTH IN SCHOOLS AND COLLEGES (DFE, AUGUST 2017).	· SURVEY AND CASE STUDIES ABOUT SCHOOL ACTIVITIES TO SUPPORT PUPILS' MENTAL HEALTH AND WELL-BEING.	· DRAW UPON RELEVANT EVIDENCE TO SUPPORT AND INFORM YOUR OWN PRACTICE.

❖ Critical questions

1. How well do you understand the picture of children's mental health and well-being in your school?

2. What issues may be impacting on the mental health and well-being of the children in your class?

3. What has been done in your school to ensure early recognition and intervention of potential mental health issues?

4. What will you do to enhance early detection and intervention of mental health issues in your setting?

5. What does your school do to effectively look after children's mental health?

6. What are your key priorities to enhance the effectiveness of how you look after children's mental health?

7. How consistent is your school's approach to mental health? How do you know? How might this be enhanced?

8. After reading this chapter, can you identify any children who you may need to consider in relation to their mental health? Why? Who might support you with this?

9. Were there any issues that you had previously not linked to potential mental health issues?

10. How visible is mental health as an issue within your curriculum?

11. How do you support children in managing academic pressures? What impact has this had? How might this be further enhanced?

12. How do you support children and their families in managing pressures that may be associated with homework?

13. How well do you engage children in considering what mental health is in a balanced manner?

14. How do you ensure a consistent approach between teachers and parents and carers when dealing with these issues? How might this be enhanced?

15. To what extent is mental health destigmatised in your school? How has this been achieved?

16. Which elements of your mental health curriculum are strengths and which require development? Refer to the eight principles to support your thinking and reflection here.

17. Do you mark Mental Health Week in your school? If so, what has worked well? If not, how might you begin to work on this?

18. How will you develop and embed empathy within and across your curriculum?

19. Which aspects of active listening are your strengths, and which would benefit from development?

20. How effectively do you develop children's emotional intelligence?

21. Do you deploy any features of the growth mindset approach? What are the benefits and how might possible limitations be overcome?

22. How confident are you in understanding how to address issues around attachment?

further reading and resources

Centre for Mental Health (www. centreformentalhealth.org.uk/our-work/ children-families)	A range of information and research concerning mental health. The Children and Families section includes some particularly useful information and guidance.
Young Minds (https://youngminds.org.uk)	A range of online resources to support professionals alongside a parents' helpline.
Mentally Healthy Schools (Heads Together) (www.mentallyhealthyschools. org.uk)	A range of good-quality information, advice and resources to support primary schools in better understanding and promoting mental health. This is specifically aimed at primary schools, and the resources are constantly being updated.
Place 2 Be (www.place2be.org.uk/our-story/why-our-work-matters)	An organisation that focuses on providing early help regarding mental health.
Anna Freud National Centre for Children and Families (www.annafreud.org)	A children's mental health charity.
World Mental Health Day (Mental Health Foundation) (www.mentalhealth.org.uk/ campaigns/world-mental-health-day)	World Mental Health Day takes place on 10 October each year. This website contains a range of resources to promote positive talk about mental health, including within schools.
Action for Happiness (www. actionforhappiness.org)	A range of resources and ideas about how we can all take action to promote happiness. There are also a range of apps, which support some of the suggested actions, including 'Three Good Things: A Happiness Journal' which encourages users (from Key Stage 2) to consider three positive things that have happened to them that day.
Headspace for Kids (www.headspace. com/meditation/kids)	This website focuses on the use of meditation to promote lifelong positive mental health. There is also an app, suitable from Key Stages 1–2 that promotes calm, focus and good sleep habits.

PSHE Association (www.pshe-association. org.uk/curriculum-and-resources/ resources/guidance-preparing-teach- about-mental-health-and)	This provides guidance on how to teach about mental health and emotional well-being.
NAHT resources (www.naht.org.uk/news- and-opinion/news/pupil-well-being-news/ youre-never-too-young-to-talk-mental- health-free-teaching-resources)	Free resources based on the 'You're Never Too Young to Talk About Mental Health' campaign.
Time to Change mental-health resources for schools and parents (www.time-to- change.org.uk/get-involved/get-involved- schools/school-resources)	A range of resources to engage teachers, parents and children in talking about mental health.
BBC mental health teaching resources (www.bbc.co.uk/programmes/ articles/5QM6H01X6b3jTQF85GLgbFl/ when-i-worry-about-things)	A range of issues connected to mental health are explored through stories.
Mental Health Foundation (www. mentalhealth.org.uk/publications/ make-it-count-guide-for-teachers)	A range of resources and information to support your provision of mental health education.
Action for Children (www. actionforchildren.org.uk)	A range of information and resources related to children's mental health and well- being. This is focused on early intervention and support. It is largely aimed at parents but could certainly be of use and interest to teachers.
NSPCC Mental Health and Suicidal Thoughts (www.nspcc.org.uk/ preventing-abuse/keeping-children-safe/ mental-health-suicidal-thoughts-children)	Useful information about how to support children who are experiencing mental health problems.
Nip in the Bud (https://nipinthebud.org)	A website focused on children's mental health and well-being. This includes a range of resources including short films and fact sheets that are aimed at teachers and parents/carers. There is a focus on early recognition to ensure appropriate intervention and treatment.
Children's Mental Health Week (Place2Be) (www.childrensmentalhealthweek.org.uk)	A range of resources to support the current theme for this important week.

Lucy's Blue Day (www.lucysblueday.com)	A storybook for children with the message, 'It's OK not to be OK.'
National Institute for Health and Care Excellence (www.nice.org.uk)	This website provides links to a range of resources based on projects and associated documentation on a range of issues, for example the identification and management of depression in children and young people.
Royal College of Psychiatrists (www. rcpsych.ac.uk/members/your-faculties/ child-adolescent-psychiatry/news-and- resources/for-public)	A range of storybook suggestions for primary-aged children. The list is divided by theme to enable you to identify stories that may address particular issues individual children may be having.
The Attachment Research Community (https://the-arc.org.uk)	A range of resources and research to support schools in enhancing their awareness of issues associated with attachment and trauma to support provision and outcomes for children.
Book Trust, 13 books to help your child feel more calm and mindful (www.booktrust. org.uk/booklists/c/calming-mindfulness)	A range of books for children to support them in feeling more relaxed, mindful and happy.

References

Armiger, M (2019) Teachers Aren't Experts: They Need Tools to Talk About Mental Health. [online] Available at: www.tes.com/news/teachers-arent-experts-they-need-tools-talk-about-mental-health (accessed 20 February 2019).

Attachment Research Community (2019) *Promoting Mental Health and Well-Being through Attachment and Trauma Aware Approaches in Education.* [online] Available at: https://the-arc. org.uk (accessed 20 February 2019).

Brown, B (2013) Brené Brown on Empathy. [online] Available at: www.youtube.com/ watch?v=1Evwgu369Jw (accessed 20 February 2019).

Busch, B (2018) Research Every Teacher Should Know: Growth Mindset. [online] Available at: www.theguardian.com/teacher-network/2018/jan/04/research-every-teacher-should-know-growth-mindset (accessed 21 February 2019).

Children's Society (2016) The Damage of Debt: The Impact of Money Worries on Children's Mental Health and Well-Being. [online] Available at: www.childrenssociety.org.uk/what-we-do/ resources-and-publications/the-damage-of-debt-the-impact-of-money-worries-on-childrens (accessed 4 February 2019).

Condra, M (2013) *What Is Mental Health?* [online] Available at: www.youtube.com/watch?v=aNQBdIMM3mQ (accessed 20 February 2019).

Department for Education (2018) *Mental Health and Behaviour in Schools*, London: DfE.

Department of Health and the Department for Education (2017) Transforming Children and Young People's Mental Health Provision: A Green Paper. [online] Available at: https://assets.publishing.service.gov.uk/government/uploads/system/uploads/attachment_data/file/664855/Transforming_children_and_young_people_s_mental_health_provision.pdf (accessed 4 February 2019).

Education Support Partnership (2018) How to Support Colleagues and Students with Mental Health Issues. [online] Available at: www.educationsupportpartnership.org.uk/blogs/how-support-colleagues-and-students-mental-health-issues (accessed 20 February 2019).

FE News (2019) Exam Culture Is Impacting Mental Health Even at Primary School. [online] Available at: www.fenews.co.uk/fevoices/15420-primary-school-children-almost-as-stressed-over-exams-as-gcse-pupils (accessed 11 February 2019).

Glazzard, J and Bligh, C (2018) *Meeting the Mental Health Needs of Children 4–11 Years*. St Albans: Critical Publishing.

Glazzard, J and Bostwick, R (2018) *Positive Mental Health: A Whole School Approach*. St Albans: Critical Publishing.

Glazzard, J and Mitchell, C (2018) *Social Media and Mental Health in Schools*. St Albans: Critical Publishing.

GOV.UK (2019) One of the Largest Mental Health Trials Launches in Schools. [online] Available at: www.gov.uk/government/news/one-of-the-largest-mental-health-trials-launches-in-schools (accessed 11 February 2019).

House of Commons Committee of Public Accounts (2019) Mental Health Services for Children and Young People. [online] Available at: https://publications.parliament.uk/pa/cm201719/cmselect/cmpubacc/1593/1593.pdf (accessed 4 February 2019).

Mental Health Foundation (2018) Talking to Your Children About Scary World News. [online] Available at: www.mentalhealth.org.uk/publications/talking-to-your-children-scary-world-news (accessed 20 February 2019).

Mental Health Foundation (2019a) Children and Young People. [online] Available at: www.mentalhealth.org.uk/a-to-z/c/children-and-young-people (accessed 4 February 2019).

Mental Health Foundation (2019b) Parents and Mental Health. [online] Available at: www.mentalhealth.org.uk/a-to-z/p/parents-and-mental-health (accessed 4 February 2019).

National Society for the Prevention of Cruelty to Children (2018) *The Courage to Talk: Childline Annual Review 2017/18*, London: NSPCC.

NHS Digital (2018) Mental Health of Children and Young People in England, 2017. [online] Available at: https://digital.nhs.uk/data-and-information/publications/statistical/mental-health-of-children-and-young-people-in-england/2017/2017 (accessed 7 February 2019).

Public Health England (2015) Promoting Children and Young People's Emotional Health and Well-Being. [online] Available at: https://assets.publishing.service.gov.uk/government/uploads/system/uploads/attachment_data/file/414908/Final_EHWB_draft_20_03_15.pdf (accessed 20 February 2019).

TES (2018) SATS Pressure in Primaries Is Too Much, Say Parents. [online] Available at: www.tes.com/news/sats-pressure-primaries-too-much-say-parents (accessed 11 February 2019).

World Health Organization (2014) Mental Health: A State of Well-Being. [online] Available at: www.who.int/features/factfiles/mental_health/en/ (accessed 20 February 2019).

10. MENTAL HEALTH AND WELL-BEING FOR TEACHERS

Key issues

For a number of years, there have been concerns about the retention of teachers in the profession. Recently workload has been formally acknowledged as a factor with links to teachers' mental health and well-being. The way it is tackled in schools varies greatly. With the constant barrage of tasks, it can be incredibly difficult to manage. As Turner and Braine (2016, cited by Ovenden-Hope and Brimacombe, 2018) state: '*Teachers need to know how to look after themselves. This may seem a simple and easy task; however, when faced with a multitude of teaching tasks, one of the areas all teachers can miss, is taking care of themselves.*'

The DfE and Ofsted are aware of the extent of the issue and are taking measures to address workload, but inevitably these will take time to embed. In the proposed new Ofsted framework from September 2019, there is clear evidence of how the watchdog is taking steps to ensure inspection does not create unnecessary work for school colleagues. For example, they will not look at non-statutory internal progress and attainment data. The DfE (2019b, p

11) in the *Teacher Recruitment and Retention Strategy* notes that, '*Teacher workload is too high, and this has been a long-standing issue. But workload is not simply about number of hours worked; it is also about teachers feeling in control of their work.*'

This chapter explores the issues and considers some manageable, useful strategies to support you in managing your workload and feeling empowered to regain control, linked to key documentation.

Why is this an issue?

Workload is one of the most commonly cited drivers for teachers leaving the profession as it adversely affects their well-being. The *Teacher Well-being Index* (Education Support Partnership, 2018) notes the following:

- 67 per cent of education professionals describe themselves as stressed.
- 29 per cent of all teachers work more than fifty-one hours a week on average.
- 74 per cent of education professionals consider the inability to switch off and relax to be a major contributing factor to a negative work–life balance.
- 57 per cent of all education professionals have considered leaving the sector over the past two years as a result of health pressures.
- 72 per cent of education professionals cite workload as the main reason for considering leaving their jobs.

Stanley (2019) makes an interesting point about what teacher well-being is about:

well-being is not just about happiness. It extends to feeling challenged, having a sense of purpose and feeling a sense of achievement and contribution to society. Working in education should help to fulfil all these requirements – they're the key reasons why people enter this great profession – yet far too often the pressures of the role and the lack of support are preventing a dedicated, talented and committed generation of educators from feeling good enough.

The links between workload, well-being and mental health are inextricable. While it can be seen as the responsibility of an individual to ensure appropriate balance, external pressures play an inevitable part. At the time of writing, there is significant and wide-ranging work being done to address teacher well-being and workload, but it will take time to embed. Now is the time to embrace the documentation that is being published to support teacher workload and well-being and begin to make those changes.

Good practice example

TAKE TIME TO REFLECT ON YOUR PRACTICE IN RELATION TO WORKLOAD

Think of a task that you do regularly.

- Is this a mandatory requirement?
- If yes, what impact will this have on outcomes for children? Did it enhance outcomes?
- Was it carried out in the most effective/efficient way?
- What were the pros and cons of doing this task? (Consider your response in relation to outcomes for children and managing your own workload and well-being.)
- How might you have done this in a more effective or efficient manner?
- What could you share with colleagues in order to enhance their work–life balance?
- Does any research support your approach?

Awareness is key to helping you manage your workload and well-being. Ovenden-Hope and Brimacombe (2018) note three key elements that teachers need to manage in respect of their well-being:

1. mental and emotional: needing to respond on a personal level to the demands of other stakeholders;
2. physical: moving and talking all day;
3. social: engaging in a professional manner with the full range of stakeholders.

Key messages

It is all too easy to continue with existing ways of working without challenging them. Putting forward a challenge can be particularly difficult if you are new to a school or at an early stage of your career, but you need to put your well-being at the fore as without this you will not be the effective teacher you need and want to be.

CHANGE

By taking time to reflect on the tasks you do, you will be able to get a greater insight into their effectiveness. If you are doing something that you believe is not being done in the most efficient or effective way, change it. It can sometimes seem that the change is just about making your life easier, but you also need to consider the potential impact of the task on outcomes for children. If it doesn't improve outcomes, change it. As Holmes (2019, p 49) states, '*We have to be ruthless, though. Every task needs to justify its position on our to-do list.*'

KEEP

So far, this chapter seems to have just talked about change. There will be many tasks that you do efficiently and that have a positive impact on pupil outcomes. These should be kept, and it is also important to think about how such effective practice can be shared or disseminated to a wider audience of teachers. The strategy may seem simple on the surface, but it is often the simplest of ideas that proves to be the most effective. In this way you are assisting with the well-being of others.

STOP

It would be very easy to spend every hour working trying to achieve the perfect lesson plan, but this is not going to make you the most effective in the classroom. Inevitably, early in your career, lesson planning will take longer, but this needs to be focused on outcomes for children rather than scripting every word you say. Ovenden-Hope and Brimacombe (2018) emphasise that, '*if the evidence base suggests that the tasks in your lesson plan will support student progress then that is good enough. Stop there.* ' It is tempting to continue the search for the ultimate and most perfect resource, which in reality may not exist, so keep a handle on what will do the job and stop to make time for you.

RECOGNISE THE MYTHS

Ofsted, for a number of years, has produced a document called the 'Myth Buster' which seeks to challenge the misconceptions surrounding Ofsted's expectations. These myths still appear to be prevalent in schools and need to be addressed so that progress can be made. The key points from this document related to your workload are as follows.

- There is no requirement to provide individual lesson plans for an inspection.
- There is no expectation in terms of planning format, the amount of detail included, or the time taken to complete. The focus is on effectiveness.
- In terms of children's work, there is recognition that the amount of work in books and folders will depend on the children's age and subjects. There is no expectation of how much work will be included in books or how often this is done.
- Schools should decide about the volume, frequency and type of feedback (written or verbal) through their policy. Ofsted will check that the policy is being applied consistently.
- There is no expectation to have a written record of verbal feedback.

- There is a clear drive to ensure that any recommendations to improve marking will not add unnecessary workload burdens.
- Data will form part of the inspection, but Ofsted only expects to see the format for tracking and monitoring progress that is routinely used.
- There is often a drive to use photographic evidence of work, but this is not needed. Inspectors will use discussions with children to gain an insight into their understanding developed through the teaching.

(Ofsted, 2018)

TALK

It is all too easy to just carry on and not question working practices. If you feel that tasks are overly complicated and time-consuming or involve duplication, you must speak to someone. This can easily be done in a professional and measured way by explaining the nature of the task. It is likely that others may be having the same concerns, so speaking out has the potential to raise a concern that may otherwise go unnoticed. Discussion around workload and well-being should, ideally, be standing agenda items on any type of review you have as a teacher so that it is kept at the fore of your daily work. Staff meetings are also a good time to bring issues into the open and challenge existing practice, particularly in the light of the *Eliminating Unnecessary Workload* documents. The ultimate message stemming from all of this is summed up beautifully by Ovenden-Hope and Brimacombe (2018): '*Resilience does not mean struggling to meet unachievable workload expectations; it is about sustaining your effectiveness as a teacher.*'

Sources of support

EARLY CAREER TEACHERS

Green (2018) refers to a government study conducted by Higton et al in 2017 which found that, '*teachers in the first five years of their career worked longer hours than their more experienced peers.*' There is often confusion about what is required in terms of paperwork so clarity around this is needed, but in addition to this schools and training providers also need to carefully consider the purpose of absolutely everything trainees and early career teachers are asked to do. The DfE (2018a) has produced advice for Initial Teacher Education (ITE) providers, and it is clear that early recognition and intervention with issues concerning workload is a national priority. Key areas that the document encourages providers to consider are:

- efficiency and impact: ensuring that tasks trainees are required to complete impact upon outcomes for children and the trainee's professional development;
- effective collaboration to help trainees develop curriculum planning skills: this is to encourage collaboration in a range of forms and the evaluation and use of existing resources to support teaching;

- high-quality training and support: to ensure that providers and school colleagues can support trainees effectively in terms of workload and well-being;
- shared expectations: to ensure application of the principles stemming from the *Eliminating Unnecessary Workload* documents in relation to professional duties and to ensure proportionate approaches to the collation of evidence against the Teachers' Standards;
- support for mentors: to ensure that the workload expected of mentors supporting a trainee does not add unnecessarily to their existing workload.

The importance of talk is again central here to ensure progress is made. Without this early support and modelling of effective workload practices to support well-being, potential issues are being created for the future. As with any issue, early intervention is a very good starting point to ensure successful outcomes.

Good practice example

SETTING APPROPRIATE EXPECTATIONS FOR TRAINEES AND EARLY CAREER TEACHERS

LESSON PLANNING

Ensure that trainees use the most appropriate format. This may be one provided by the provider or the placement school. Trainees should not have to complete more than one version. Ensure that trainees focus on outcomes, eg, a sequence of lessons, rather than overly detailed individual lesson plans.

RESOURCING

Encourage trainees to utilise resources that already exist rather than reinventing the wheel. Encourage collaboration with colleagues to generate and share effective resources. Provide a facility, such as cloud-based storage to enable wider sharing of effective resources and also facilitate access to a broader range to reduce time finding resources at the planning stage.

USE OF NON-CONTACT TIME

Ensure that non-contact time is carefully planned and includes appropriate CPD opportunities. Engage trainees in regular and purposeful discussions, based on their practice, about the *Eliminating Unnecessary Workload* documents.

ASSESSMENT OF TRAINEES

Ensure these discussions focus on workload; for example in addition to discussing the quality of planning, also take time to consider the time taken to complete this.

PLACEMENT EXPECTATIONS

Ensure that these are realistic and appropriate given the stage of their training and career and how relevant the expectations are in terms of the impact the tasks will have on the children and the trainee's professional progress. Consider the necessity or unnecessity of tasks in relation to the potential impact on outcomes for pupils.

These principles could easily be applied to more experienced teachers. Take time to reflect on practice, engaging with all relevant stakeholders, and challenge everything where workload could potentially be eased to enhance trainee well-being and retention in the profession.

THE EARLY CAREER FRAMEWORK

The DfE released *The Early Career Framework* in January 2019 with a view to national implementation from September 2021. This document has resulted from early career teachers not having the time to dedicate to their professional development. This is a two-year package of structured training and support. The importance of having time to do this and not creating extra workload are key features of the document. It focuses on five key areas:

1. behaviour management;
2. pedagogy;
3. curriculum;
4. assessment; and
5. professional behaviours.

There are positive plans in terms of workload which will see the 10 per cent NQT (newly qualified teacher) time remain and then 5 per cent non-contact time in the second year of teaching and funding to allow mentors time to support early career teachers.

RESEARCH-INFORMED APPROACHES

With constant flux in the educational landscape, it is often difficult to know how best to implement new initiatives in the most effective manner. The EEF has independently assessed and approved the underpinning evidence of the Early Career Framework. The work of the EEF should be used to inform your approaches and could potentially save time in not reinventing the wheel. While tweaks may need to be made to suit your particular context, the overarching principles will support the implementation of new ways of working or endorse what you already do as good practice. The document refers to a wealth of research publications but usefully asterisks those which are recommended; another useful way to support the management of your workload.

TEACHER RECRUITMENT AND RETENTION

In early 2019, the DfE published its *Teacher Recruitment and Retention Strategy.* Throughout the four priorities, there is a clear sense of the need to address issues around workload and well-being.

1. More supportive school cultures and reduced workload. The DfE and Ofsted are working together to reduce unnecessary pressures placed on teachers by accountability measures. It also highlights that the new Ofsted framework will emphasise workload reduction.

2. Transforming support for early career teachers. A reduced timetable for early career teachers in their first two years to facilitate effective professional development opportunities.

3. Making sure teaching remains an attractive career as lifestyles and aspirations change. Introducing easier ways to facilitate flexible working, including the launch of a job-share service.

4. Making it easier for great people to become teachers by simplifying the application process.

It will be interesting to see how this works in practice, but again it seems that now is the time to start considering how change may be instigated in your setting. It is important to challenge what has gone before and to seek more effective, streamlined and efficient ways of working.

WORKLOAD TOOLKIT

The DfE published the *Workload Reduction Toolkit* in July 2018. This is based on a three-stage approach to self-evaluation:

1. Identifying the workload issues in your school. This enables schools to pinpoint specific areas requiring development or attention.

2. Addressing the workload issues in your school. A range of links to resources are provided to support schools with this.

3. Evaluating the impact.

The resource also includes case studies of effective practice in terms of reducing workload in key areas to support other schools in adapting their practice. Ofsted will have a keen interest in how this resource has been used to enhance the workload of staff in your school. Included as part of the resource is a poster and a pamphlet that summarise key points relating to key aspects of workload. These usefully identify what is best practice and relate this to Ofsted expectations. It is important that there is regular and meaningful discussion with all staff about the key aspects of this work and the associated documents in order to enhance practice and outcomes in terms of teacher workload.

PLANNING AND TEACHING RESOURCES

The Independent Teacher Workload Review Group (ITWRG, 2016c) emphasises the importance of planning but notes that this is where teachers can spend excessive amounts of their time. It is important that you take time to reflect upon the purpose of planning with the Group, noting that: *'Too often, "planning" refers to the production of daily written lesson plans which function as proxy evidence for an accountability "paper trail" rather than the process of effective planning for pupil progress and attainment.'*

The focus on collaboration at the planning stage is further reinforced as is the need to utilise existing good-quality resources rather than reinventing the wheel. A key component needed, particularly in relation to the collaboration element is time, and this is something that may need to be considered more creatively in your setting. Five principles came from this piece of work, which again may be helpful in structuring your reflections on the planning processes deployed:

1. Planning a sequence of lessons is more important than writing individual lesson plans.

2. Fully resourced schemes of work should be in place for all teachers to use each term.

3. Planning should not be done simply to please outside organisations.

4. Planning should take place in purposeful and well-defined blocks of time.

5. Effective planning makes use of high-quality resources.

The ITWRG (2016c) notes the work of Hattie (2012) who states that:

Planning can be done in many ways, but the most powerful is when teachers work together to develop plans, develop common understandings of what is worth teaching, collaborate on understanding their beliefs of challenge and progress, and work together to evaluate the impact of their planning on student outcome.

MARKING

Marking is always the thing that one hears teachers speaking less than positively about. This often stems from teachers not seeing the value in what they do. The 'Eliminating Unnecessary Workload Around Marking' document (ITWRG, 2016b) makes the distinction between quantity and quality of feedback. The idea of working the longest hours to be the best teacher seems to be a common misconception here. The following statement from the document should make you stop and think about practice, particularly if you spend excessive time on providing written feedback: *'In particular, we are concerned that it has become common practice for teachers to provide extensive written comments on every piece of work when there is little evidence that this improves pupil outcomes in the long term.'*

As with anything in teaching, there is not a universal approach that will fit every situation, but the marking that is required should be appropriate to the age of the children and the stage of the learning for any given subject.

The three principles of effective marking stemming from the work of the ITWRG (2016b) are that it should be:

1. meaningful – the teacher needs to decide what is most appropriate in terms of supporting pupil progress and outcomes;

2. manageable – feedback can take a range of forms, but it should be considered in terms of the impact the marking has on progress; if it is taking too long, changes to practice should be made;

3. motivational – acknowledge and celebrate the children's efforts and achievements; consider how this may be done without excessive marking.

DATA MANAGEMENT

Data management is another aspect of the job which is either loved or hated. It is the purpose of the data that needs to be considered with care not merely collected. It is noted by the ITWRG (2016a) that workload around data is increased when it is the collection that is the main focus, whereas it should be on *'the core purpose of improving outcomes for pupils.'* The common principles identified by the group are as follows.

- Be streamlined and eliminate duplication.
- Be ruthless: always consider why the data is required.
- Be prepared to stop: avoid carrying on with what has always been done if it is not effective.
- Be aware of workload issues.

All of these documents will inevitably provide some food for thought in terms of practice in school. The tools are there to support you, but there needs to be space for these discussions about the purpose of tasks, the efficiency of the tasks and the reliability and validity of the data produced as a result.

Summary

As you know, workload is a complex issue that has been a concern for many years. Now we are in a position where this is widely acknowledged, and work is being done to address it. It will take time, and there are no easy answers, but constant consideration of priorities and the potential impact of practices is needed to move things forward. You need to be mindful of your commitments and ensure that the deadlines set for and by you are achievable. Most importantly, you need to ensure you have time for you so that you can be productive in all aspects of your work. With so much to do, this can be hard, but making the time is well worth the effort. Often tasks can seem insurmountable, but consider how collaborating with colleagues can support you in finding a manageable bite-sized way forward.

Policy summary

POLICY	KEY POINTS	IMPLICATIONS FOR SCHOOLS
OFSTED 2019 FRAMEWORK	• STAFF WORKLOAD WILL BE CONSIDERED AS PART OF THE LEADERSHIP AND MANAGEMENT JUDGEMENT. SCHOOLS WHO UTILISE PRACTICES, SUCH AS FOR THE PURPOSE OF DATA MANAGEMENT, WHICH ARE BURDENSOME WILL NOT ACHIEVE HIGHLY.	• ENSURE THAT ALL POLICIES, PROCEDURES AND WORKING PRACTICES HAVE BEEN CAREFULLY CONSIDERED IN RELATION TO THE IMPACT OF WORKLOAD. • BE CLEAR ABOUT HOW RELEVANT RESOURCES, INCLUDING THE DFE WORKLOAD TOOLKIT HAVE INFORMED YOUR APPROACHES.
EARLY CAREER FRAMEWORK (DFE, 2019)	• A TWO-YEAR PACKAGE OF SUPPORT FOR EARLY CAREER TEACHERS TO ENSURE TIME IS DEDICATED TO THEIR PROFESSIONAL DEVELOPMENT. NATIONAL ROLLOUT WILL BE FROM SEPTEMBER 2021.	• CONSIDER PRACTICAL IMPLICATIONS IN PREPARATION. • IDENTIFY ASPECTS OF GOOD PRACTICE RELATED TO EARLY CAREER DEVELOPMENT OPPORTUNITIES WHICH COULD BE BUILT UPON IN LIGHT OF THIS.

POLICY	KEY POINTS	IMPLICATIONS FOR SCHOOLS
WORKLOAD REDUCTION TOOLKIT (DFE, 2018)	• THIS PROVIDES PRACTICAL ADVICE AND RESOURCES TO SUPPORT SCHOOL SELF-EVALUATION AND REVIEW OF PRACTICE WITH A VIEW TO REDUCING WORKLOAD.	• ENGAGE WITH THE RESOURCE TO PINPOINT SPECIFIC AREAS WITHIN YOUR SCHOOL THAT REQUIRE WORK. • USE THE RESOURCES PROVIDED TO SUPPORT DEVELOPMENT AND THEN EVALUATE THE IMPACT IN ORDER TO IDENTIFY ANY NECESSARY NEXT STEPS. • CONSIDER HOW THIS COULD BE USED TO SHOW OFSTED EVIDENCE OF PROACTIVE AND MEANINGFUL ENGAGEMENT WITH THE WORKLOAD AGENDA.

❖ Critical questions

1. How well do you look after yourself? What could you do to improve this?

2. What are the best parts of your job and which aspects make you feel negatively about teaching? What might you do to address the negative aspects?

3. Which external pressures have a particular impact on you?

4. Do you ever take time to reflect upon your practice in relation to workload? How might doing this help you and your colleagues?

5. Are there any existing ways of working which you feel need to be challenged in order to improve workload?

6. How could you justify any changes that need to be made to senior leaders?

7. What are you currently doing that is working well and impacts positively on your workload and well-being?

8. How do or could you disseminate effective practice to colleagues to enhance their workload and well-being?

9. What are the strengths of your approach to lesson planning and how could you enhance this?

10. Did you hold any misconceptions about Ofsted expectations prior to reading this chapter? How have they been addressed?

11. Based on your understanding of Ofsted myths, are there any aspects of your practice which you could change to achieve a positive impact on your workload?

12. How confident do you feel to talk to relevant colleagues about workload concerns? What do you feel more able to do as a result of this chapter?

13. How might your time be better organised to support your professional development needs?

14. Which principles related to trainee and early career teachers do you feel are your strengths and which aspects of your practice will require further development?

15. To what extent do you use evidence-informed approaches? What impact has this had on your workload and outcomes for children?

16. What do you consider to be the benefits of drawing upon evidence-informed approaches in terms of your workload?

17. What issues might arise around workload when drawing on evidence-informed approaches? How might these be overcome?

18. Before using the Workload Reduction Toolkit, consider what the workload issues are in your school and how they may be overcome. It will be interesting to see how your feelings compare.

19. How well are the *Eliminating Unnecessary Workload* documents used to inform and drive changes to policy and practice in your school? What impact have these had? What might the next steps be?

further reading and resources

Schoolwell (http://schoolwell.co.uk)	A website containing a range of ideas and resources to support staff well-being.
Education Support Partnership (www. educationsupportpartnership.org.uk)	A range of research and ideas to support the well-being of teachers.

TES Teacher Well-Being (www.tes.com/news/hub/teacher-wellbeing)	Articles exploring issues around teacher well-being and strategies to support this.
Young Minds: Caring for the Well-Being of Teachers and School Staff (https://youngminds.org.uk/resources/school-resources/caring-for-the-wellbeing-of-teachers-and-school-staff)	Guidance on enhancing the well-being of teachers.
The Guardian: Teacher Well-Being (www.theguardian.com/teacher-network/series/teacher-wellbeing-2014)	Articles exploring issues around teacher well-being.
Anna Freud Centre for Children and Families, 'Ten Steps Towards School Staff Well-Being' (www.annafreud.org/what-we-do/schools-in-mind/resources-for-schools/ten-steps-towards-school-staff-wellbeing)	Based on a survey of teachers, this is a resource containing materials and guidance to support reflection about staff well-being with a view to impacting positively on children's mental health.
Anna Freud Centre for Children and Families, 'Schools in Mind' (www.annafreud.org/what-we-do/schools-in-mind)	This is a free network to share a range of ideas concerning well-being and mental health in schools. It includes a range of resources.
Mental Health at Work (www.mentalhealthatwork.org.uk)	A website containing a range of ideas to enhance working conditions with a focus on mental health.
Mindful Teachers (www.mindfulteachers.org)	A range of ideas to promote well-being based on the notion of mindfulness.
NHS, 'Five Steps to Improve Mental Well-Being' (www.nhs.uk/conditions/stress-anxiety-depression/improve-mental-wellbeing)	Practical strategies to promote and improve mental health and well-being.
National Education Union Workload Campaign (https://neu.org.uk/campaigns/workload-campaign)	Includes a toolkit to help reduce teacher workload, with three sections: (1) identify the issues; (2) address the issues; (3) evaluate the impact.
Gumbrell, D (2019) *Lift! Going Up If Teaching Gets You Down*. St Albans: Critical Publishing (www.criticalpublishing.com/lift)	This is a practical text aimed at all levels of teacher to promote individual reflection or wider staff discussion about resilience and well-being.
Price, S (2019) *Essential Guides for Early Careers Teachers: Mental Well-Being and Self-Care*, edited by E Hollis. St Albans: Critical Publishing.	This is a quick-read about mental well-being and self-care for all early-career teachers.

References

Department for Education (2018a) *Addressing Workload in Initial Teacher Education (ITE)*. London: DfE.

Department for Education (2018b) Workload Reduction Toolkit. [online] Available at: www.gov.uk/government/collections/workload-reduction-toolkit (accessed 21 February 2019).

Department for Education (2019a) *Early Career Framework*. London: DfE.

Department for Education (2019b) *Teacher Recruitment and Retention Strategy*. London: DfE.

Education Support Partnership (2018) Teacher Well-Being Index 2018. [online] Available at: www.educationsupportpartnership.org.uk/resources/research-reports/teacher-wellbeing-index-2018 (accessed 21 February 2019).

Green, M (2018) Supporting Your Workload As an Early Career Teacher. [online] Available at: https://impact.chartered.college/article/green-supporting-workload-early-career-teacher/ (accessed 21 February 2019).

Hattie, J (2012) *Visible Learning for Teachers, Maximising Impact on Learning,* Abingdon: Routledge (pp 67–74)

Holmes, E (2019) *A Practical Guide to Teacher Well-Being*. London: Sage.

Independent Teacher Workload Review Group (2016a) Eliminating Unnecessary Workload Associated with Data Management. [online] Available at: https://assets.publishing.service.gov.uk/government/uploads/system/uploads/attachment_data/file/511258/Eliminating-unnecessary-workload-associated-with-data-management.pdf (accessed 21 February 2019).

Independent Teacher Workload Review Group (2016b) Eliminating Unnecessary Workload Around Marking. [online] Available at: https://assets.publishing.service.gov.uk/government/uploads/system/uploads/attachment_data/file/511256/Eliminating-unnecessary-workload-around-marking.pdf (accessed 21 February 2019).

Independent Teacher Workload Review Group (2016c) Eliminating Unnecessary Workload Around Planning and Teaching Resources. [online] Available at: https://assets.publishing.service.gov.uk/government/uploads/system/uploads/attachment_data/file/511257/Eliminating-unnecessary-workload-around-planning-and-teaching-resources.pdf (accessed 21 February 2019).

Ofsted (2018) Ofsted Inspections: Myths. [online] Available at: www.gov.uk/government/publications/school-inspection-handbook-from-september-2015/ofsted-inspections-mythbusting (accessed 21 February 2019).

Ovenden-Hope, T and Brimacombe, K (2018) Teacher Well-Being and Workload: Why a Work-Life Balance Is Essential for the Teaching Profession. [online] Available at: https://impact.chartered.college/article/ovenden-hope-etal-teacher-wellbeing-workload-why-work-life-balance-essential-teaching-profession/ (accessed 21 February 2019).

Stanley, J (2019) We Must Change Our Definition of Teacher Well-Being. [online] Available at: www.tes.com/news/we-must-change-our-definition-teacher-wellbeing (accessed 21 February 2019).

INDEX

INDEX